A FAMILY LIVING IN DARKNESS

A FAMILY LIVING IN DARKNESS

FROM THE STREETS TO THE CORNERSTONE

WILLIAM VARGAS

TATE PUBLISHING
AND ENTERPRISES, LLC

Published by Tate Publishing & Enterprises, LLC
127 E. Trade Center Terrace | Mustang, Oklahoma 73064 USA
1.888.361.9473 | www.tatepublishing.com

Tate Publishing is committed to excellence in the publishing industry. The company reflects the philosophy established by the founders, based on Psalm 68:11,
"The Lord gave the word and great was the company of those who published it."

Cover design by Nikolai Purpura
Interior design by Mary Jean Archival

Published in the United States of America

ISBN: 978-1-63063-463-6
1. Biography & Autobiography / Personal Memoirs
2. Family & Relationships / General
14.02.26

IN MEMORY OF

Norma Luz Vargas (Luz, sister)
Carmelo Vargas Maldonado (Juan del Carmen/Juan Carmelo, father)
Jose Vargas (Cheche, brother)
Carmelo Vargas Jr. (Kato, brother)
Lourdes Vargas (Lulu, sister)

and

For the living members of my family:

Maria M. Vargas (Chefa, Josephina, Josefa, mother)
Carmen Maria Vargas (Mary, sister)
William Vargas (Willie, myself)
Annette Vargas (Anne, sister)

ACKNOWLEDGMENTS

First of all, I would like to thank my Lord God and his Son Jesus for the gift and the ability he has given me to write this book. It had been about a year or so that the Holy Spirit had been dealing with me about writing our family's story, and for that I thank him. On my own accord, I would have never written this book. Because of what God has done in my personal life, I felt compelled to go ahead and write this true story. Therefore, I give God all the glory. Father God, thank You for the marvelous gift you have given me and the ability to write (James 1:17).

Also, I would like to take this opportunity to show my gratitude and my many thanks to the Church of Christ in New Jersey and in Texas for helping me in prayer for the anointing and for the writing of this book—thank you. I like to thank my wife, Barbara Vargas, for being supportive and for helping me in prayer and all our other friends who prayed with us—thank you. I also like to thank those men and women God used to guide me to Tate Publishing—thank you. Most of all, I like to thank Tate Publishing for believing in me, for publishing my story and for adding me on as a new author—thank you so much! Barbara and I asked the Lord for his anointing and that words written in this book would touch the hearts of many souls across the United States of America and abroad.

Once again, thank you all. I give all the glory to God and to his Son, Jesus Christ, the savior of the world. Hallelujah, praise God!

I acknowledged with my deepest and sincerest gratitude the influence the Church of Christ has had on my personal life after all these many years since I've been saved. I given my life to God via Jesus Christ at age twenty-five and have no regrets. Living God's way has been the best life I've ever lived. He has given me a life of hope, faith, and love in his Son, Jesus Christ. Therefore, above all things, I thank him for all he's done for me and my family. Thank you, Father. You are great!

CONTENTS

FOREWORD

This book is based on a true story. There's much to say about living in the "ghettos" of Newark, New Jersey. Many families living in Newark and abroad the United States have been victimized with the pain and hurts that the abused of drugs, alcohol, guns, murders, and all sorts of crimes have inflicted on them. Many of these families still find themselves lost without any hope and will never be able to move on from their existing environment, without the assistance and encouragement of others. It is from this intent that I bring my story to you. As I present this book, it is my deepest desire that you too can have a chance at life and understand that there's always a way out with Jesus. Christ is the answer for all your problems. He can help you escape free from the strongholds of your environment. Satan has kept many poor families bound by his evil darts, but I'm here to tell you that Jesus can deliver you from the devil's demonic schemes. It is written in the New Testament, "Then you will know the truth, and the truth will set you free" (John 8:32 NIV).

It is my desire to write nothing but truth and to bring you to the knowledge of the only Son of God, Jesus Christ. You will always find hope, faith, and love in him and may the Holy Spirit bring conviction to your lives as you read along the lines and pages of this book. May God's blessing be upon you and your families, and may the Lord Jesus keep you under his protection. I pray that this book helps direct your lives to the reading of the Holy Scriptures, where you can find the key of your salvation, i.e., Christ. It is to him that we should focus our attention (Hebrews 12:2).

INTRODUCTION

This is the true story of a semireligious mother, an alcoholic father, and their seven children living in an environment full of drugs, alcohol, sex, crimes, sorceries, murders, guns, and in a desperate need of a savior while living in the ghettos of New Jersey. My family and I went through some serious hardships living in the projects known as Columbus Homes and Otto Kretchmer Homes Housing Authority. Although, our lives first started to changed while we were living in Paterson, New Jersey. This is a powerful and an emotional story with mixed feelings and sentiments but ends with a happy ending. Enjoy!

This book is about a "family living in darkness." It's a story of a family's chaos and their many problems. It's about a family who was losing the battle against all evil forces without any kind of hope, faith, or love from the most important person in the universe, i.e., God, their Creator. It's about a family who lived in constant danger, drama, and death. It's also about this family's life of darkness at the mercy of the Lord's feet. My intentions are pure, sincere, and honest. To the best of my ability, I write to you, being compelled by the Holy Spirit about me and my family, i.e., this branch of the Vargas Family. It's about a family growing up in the ghettos of New Jersey without the love of God and his Son, Jesus Christ. I like to express to you that I'm not writing fiction, but a true story about a family living in deep sins blinded by the darkness that surrounded them. It's a story addressed to give you a message. It's a "message from God." A family without God is a family lost in the world and bound by the spiritual chains of dark powers. It's about a family headed into destruction influence by drugs, alcohol, sorcery, sex, and etc. It's a desperate family in need of a savior, i.e., Jesus Christ, and during the course of time, God would turn everything around for them, even in the midst of evil.

This story is to inform you that even within your darkest hour in the midst of your life, there is a God who hears from his throne. All you need to do is call his name. Jesus still saves among the good and the bad. It doesn't matter where you come from, your background, ethnicity, religion, or political status. Jesus Christ loves you and died for you on the cross two thousand years ago. God wants you to be saved and ready for Jesus's coming.

My sole purpose in writing this story is to show what happens to a family who lives their lives without God and without the love of Jesus. In no way is my story written to expose the sins of my family, including my very own, or to judge and/or condemn any of them. I leave that to God. My main objective is to win souls for Christ, and to do that, I had to write certain things about us in order to show the world what happens when we choose to live in darkness and without the love of God. As I write my story, I exposed the deeds of Satan by saying the truth, and by letting the world know that God delivers us from darkness when Jesus becomes Lord of our lives. The story it's written to help you understand that evil forces are at work today against our lives, but that through Christ Jesus we can defeat Satan, and his demonic forces that rise against us and our families.

My story is written to bring you conviction and to cause you to react positively and follow fervently after the Lord Jesus, the Messiah. All for the glory of God and Jesus's blood cleanses us from all sin (1 John 1:7), therefore, I implore you to keep your focus on Christ and not on the characters of each person. I pray this story helps you reflect on your personal life, and that you will make Jesus Christ your Lord and savior.

Let's not forget the story of Noah in the Bible (Genesis 9:20–27). It tells us that Noah had gotten drunk and that one of his sons, i.e., Ham, had seen his father's nakedness and went and told his two brothers: Shem and Japheth. Instead of covering his father's nakedness, he exposed it by telling his brothers. Once Noah became aware of Ham's actions, he cursed his descendants.

My point in this story is that we shouldn't be exposing the sins of our parents to the world. Instead of doing that, we should be praying for them and asking God to protect them and help them keep their reputations. Parents aren't perfect and neither are we, their children. I am not saying that we should condone their sins, but that we shouldn't be saying things that will incriminate them, hurt them, or embarrass them, especially in front of others. It is considered disrespectful to our parents, and God doesn't like it at all. God has given us parents to raise us, to protect us, and to look after our well being as we grow in statute and maturity, and become independent.

God judges all sins, so let's leave that part to him and find salvation for our souls via Jesus Christ. It is written in the New Testament, "Salvation is found in no one else, for there is no other name under heaven given to men by which we must be saved" (Acts 4:12, NIV).

-1-

HOW MY PARENTS MET

My parents were born and raised in the Island of Puerto Rico which is Commonwealth with United States of America.

My Dad was born in 1925 and came from a wealthy family from the town of Bo. Quebrada, Camuy, Puerto Rico where his parents owned their own business and trade. His dad had lots of land and was well known in Puerto Rico, not only for being a business man, but for being generous. Most of all, he was known for his political influences in the community. His involvement in politics won him favor with the people of his village and the town municipality. My Dad was the oldest of twelve siblings and as a young boy growing up in the sugar cane fields of Puerto Rico, he learned early to work the farms. The family had plenty of cows, chickens, mules, horses and goats to attend to in abundance. Dad loved playing the "Parachute Elite Guitars Puerto Rican Style Cuatro Acoustic Guitar. This type of guitar is made up of ten strings (five double strings to play); and Dad also loved singing.

My mom was born in 1928 and came from the town of Hatillo, but resided at Bo. Bayaney, Puerto Rico at the time of her marriage. Her childhood wasn't so great, as my Dad's, but she survived. She is the oldest of ten siblings, though her mom had taken in another six children and raised them as her own.

Altogether, there were sixteen children that my grandmother had been raising, though I suspect she had taken more in.

How did my Dad and Mom meet? Well the story is, as I know it (at least that's what my Mom told me many years ago), that she sung for a radio station for about seven years in the town of Arecibo and one day my dad heard her singing while listening to the radio. Dad decided that he wanted to know who this beautiful young lady was with such a lovely voice? Indeed, she captivated his heart with her voice. I guess she must have sung well for him to be taken by her beautiful voice. Dad made it his business to drive by the radio station where she was singing and met my Mom there. One thing led to another, they fell in love and got married. It was love at first sight. My parents were a good looking couple and were good for each other.

Mom and Dad were married in the town of Arecibo, Puerto Rico on November 28, 1949 at 5:00 PM. Mom was twenty-one and Dad was twenty-four at the time of their marriage.

During the early 1950's my parents migrated to the United States from Puerto Rico to the state of Florida with my two sisters: Mary and Luz. Two years after living in Florida they left for Newark, New Jersey. Employment in Florida wasn't that great so they decided to leave. Newark was booming with employment and Dad found work there, and Mom stayed home with the girls. Mary was the firstborn and afterwards, Luz was born. After settling in Newark, my parents had another five children born to them in Martland Hospital (now known as University Hospital), and with Mary and Luz, we totaled seven siblings: Mary, Luz, Cheche, Lulu, Kato, myself and Anne. We were four sisters and three brothers; the Vargas'.

-2-

MY CHILDHOOD YEARS

It is April of 1961, and I just had my third birthday party—hallelujah! I still remembered it as if it was yesterday. I was wearing a beautiful black and white outfit with a bow tie, then I was posing in front of the camera in front of my birthday cake. "*Gosh, what a big delicious cake*," I thought to myself. I was dying to put my teeth into it. Yummy! My family had taken a few photo shots of me and my dad.

One day, while I was still three years old, I climbed up on the small bathroom sink, i.e., on the vanity, opened the small mirror door to the medicine cabinet, and grabbed my father's razor blade and tried shaving with it. Next thing you know, I cut my face with his blade, and blood is pouring down my facial cheeks. What was I thinking? Ouch, ouch, and ouch! I don't remember if back than there were such things as throwaway razors; I only remembered grabbing the small little blade and cutting myself with it as I am bleeding, crying, worried and scared to death. My heart is pounding against my chest like one hundred miles an hour; I run to my mother's arms for comfort, all drenched in blood and just couldn't stop crying. My face turned pale. I had no clue what I was doing. The only thing I knew was that I had seen my father shaving earlier that morning, and so I decided I was gonna do the same thing he was doing because I wanted to be like him.

The things we do when growing up as children; we want to do everything we see our parents do, and we want to be just like them. Our innocent minds know no boundaries. That's why it's so important that parents do right by their children and give them the good example. You just never know what your child is thinking or is gonna do after your child has observed you. Mom had become extremely nervous after seeing me all drenched in blood. Blood was pouring all over my face and clothing. Petrified as she was, she acted immediately, ran to the bathroom's medicine cabinet, and grabbed the first aid kit. She cleaned me up, put on the bandage, and then scolded me a little and asked me questions. Of course, her questions weren't really questions; she was just nervous from what had happened to me. Then she asked, "Son, what possessed you to climb up the bathroom vanity, and why did you take your father's razor blade and try shaving with it, you have no facial hair and you're but a little boy, right?"

"Mom," I said, "I wanted to be just like Dad. I saw him shaving with the razor blade and thought that I too can shave, just like daddy did."

Mom wasn't too sure how Dad was gonna react, but she knew that the minute he got in from work and saw me with the bandage on my face, he would be highly upset. She knew he wasn't gonna take it well. Mom knew Dad's character really well.

Dad was strict in his ways, and sometimes he had a mean character about him, though he was a very nice man and a good dad. By this time, Mom and Dad had been married to each other about fifteen years. Mom knew all hell would break loose. Back then, my dad worked three different shifts. He constantly had to rotate shifts. One week he would work the day shift, the second week the evening shift, and the third week the late night shift and worked to the early morning hours. He worked in a factory and worked very hard to support the family. Dad loved his family.

Mom, still upset that I had cut myself with Dad's blade and nervous about what Dad was gonna say to her, she decides just to stay calm, sits on the couch, and thinks about what she will say to Dad the minute he walks in through the door. It was a deep cut and I bled quite a bit, but Mom managed to get it all under control. When Dad arrived from work, she was less nervous and knew exactly what she was going to tell him. Mom didn't have a car, so she waited on Dad to see what he wanted to do. They both took me to the hospital, and thank God, no stitches were needed. The hospital doctor probably gave me a tetanus shot to avoid an infection, and thank God, I was sent back home. All is well, we left the hospital and Dad drove us back home. Dad wasn't as upset as Mom first thought, just a little. He said a few things to her but didn't freak out like Mom had thought.

I was about five when we were all living in the Christopher Columbus Homes (CCH). These were high-story buildings and were better known as the Seventh Avenue projects located in Newark, New Jersey. They were fairly good to live in back then, and there were hardworking families residing in these projects. The residents living here were great neighbors; we had many friends, and together we all enjoyed life in these affordable housing projects. Everyone knew their neighbors and got along well, and respected one another. In the center of the projects was a big playground where we would all play baseball, basketball, ride bikes, and other sports. Those were the good old days when we had so much fun growing up. I went out every day with my friends or with my brother Kato and played out in the playground. We also loved playing across the street at the McKinley School playground. My brother Kato was a year older than I; whereas, my brother Cheche was four years older.

McKinley School was the very first school where both my sister Anne and I attended first grade together while Kato attended second grade. Alongside the school, to the left side was St. Lucy's Catholic Church. My mom was a devoted Catholic, and it was where we first attended church on a weekly basis as a family. Sunday's mass commenced at around 9:00 AM. Mom had attended just about all religious activities and dragged us along with her. It was something she always loved to do. During the week, the church had other activities and we attended them as well. Dad wasn't so religious, but from time to time, he too would attend church with us. Dad was from a Catholic background and came from a loving family in Puerto Rico. The church had a bingo hall and Mom loved playing bingo all the time. At times, Mom would take the three youngest of us—Kato, me, and Anne—with her to play bingo.

Dad liked having fun with his drinking buddies and with some of our family members. "Whenever he had any free time, he would invite them over, pulled out the cold beer cans from the refrigerator, and have a so-called good time playing dominoes." Dominoes were always the thing to do. Hispanic families love getting together with family and friends and play their dominoe games from the early evening hours until the late hours of the night with a few cases of six packs or eight packs of beer bottles; that's the norm. It is said among the Hispanics, that you're not Puerto Rican or Hispanic until you own your own set of dominoes to play with at your own homes when company comes over. I think that's true for most Hispanics.

There were other things the family would do for fun like going to the park for festivities, carnivals, and games. While living in Seventh Avenue projects, every year, St. Lucy's Church celebrated St. Gerald's Italian Carnival Feast Celebration. The festival lasted for a week. I remembered how good the Italians made the zeppoles. Their zeppoles were so good that I couldn't get enough zeppoles to satisfy me. Metaphorically speaking, they were to die for. They were deliciously made and everyone that went to this carnival bought and ate them. Yummy! Everyone at the festival made sure they bought at least two or three bags to take home with them after eating their first bag of zeppoles at the festival.

My family and I looked forward to this feast every year. The carnival had a bunch of rides to get on and all sorts of fun machines. My brothers, sisters, and I, along with other relatives and friends, would buy tickets for about twenty-five cents or fifty cents and up to $5, depending on the amount of rides we wanted to ride on. We must have gotten on every single ride there was to ride on. Those were very happy days and happy times for all of us, and to this day, we still cherished and have great memories that will forever stay in our hearts. The festival had live music at the carnival with all sorts of food stands. This was their annual customs, and it was amazing. The head musician was the guy who played the accordion. He played the accordion well, and the music felt like it came down from heaven. At least to me that's what it felt like. I couldn't get enough of such lovely music. It, definitely, was music to my ears. I remembered especially watching and hearing the head musician play his accordion. How ironic. Many years later, I ended up playing with a professional accordion musician at a church in New Jersey and for many years. He played very well and was a great musician. After a few years into the church, he became my pastor. Not until I started writing this book, I had not realized how God had already been working in my life via the musical accordion. God is amazing and works in mysterious ways, ways that we can't even fathom, but all his ways are good. Who would have known? Only God—hallelujah!

I was the youngest of the boys, and my sister Anne was the youngest of the girls and the youngest of all of us. Anne and I got along well, and we were very close with each other to this day. May the Lord bless her and abundantly.

Coming from a family of seven siblings was a lot of fun. Sometimes we did crazy things growing up.

One day, before we had moved out of Seventh Avenue projects, my brother Cheche and I decided to play with matches. He took the matches first and put some newspaper into a Coca-Cola bottle. He then lit the bottle with the matches and threw it out the window from our seventh-floor apartment bedroom. Then he gave me the matches and asked me to do the same. What a big mistake that was, to ask me to do the same was to ask me if I wanted candy! I lit up the newspaper he handed me and proceeded to throw it out the window, but when I got ready to throw it out, the flames almost burnt my fingers, and I dropped the newspaper on the floor near the bed. I quickly got hold of it again and threw it out the window. But neither one of us had noticed that the mattress under the bed had caught fire before I had actually grabbed the newspaper to throw it out the window. We were just trying to have fun. Suddenly, our fun turned into fear, and the bed was on fire. Next thing we know, the flames are getting out of control. Something had to be done, like really fast. We quickly rushed back and forth to the kitchen and back to the room with the biggest rice-cooking pots we could find in the kitchen cabinets. We started filling them up with water and tried to put off the fire with them, but it wasn't helping matters, and the fire was spreading fast and we just couldn't contain it.

It was around 9:00 PM by this time. If only I hadn't dropped the newspaper or if only I hadn't lit up the newspaper with the matches, I thought to myself. I was worried and so was my brother Cheche. We knew we were in big trouble. The fire spread rapidly and permeated throughout the room like a plague. We had lost complete control of the situation, and suddenly, it dawned on us what our parents had always taught us: "Do not play with matches." Just that it was a bit to late. All our efforts to put off the fire were to no avail. Before we knew it, the fire trucks and the police were at the door of our apartment. We didn't know what to do, but we knew we had to answer the door if we wanted to live and not have the rest of the apartment burn down. Had we stayed in the apartment, no doubt the fire and smoke would have suffocated us and burned us to death. Smoke was all over the apartment. Our oldest sister Mary tried helping us, but not even she was able to contain the fire because it was spreading way to fast. Mary wasn't home when the fire started. She was with Mom visiting a dear neighbor who lived on the same floor we did, and I had went over there to tell her about the fire. I was standing there all scared, telling her what had just happened and that we needed her help. She ran hysterically to the apartment and did whatever she could to help out, but it was already too late, and the situation was only getting worse by the minute. As each second pass, our lives were in danger. What a mess my brother Cheche and I had caused and what a mess we were gonna be in when our dad got in from work. Dad worked the second shift that night which was from 4:00 PM to midnight. We were expecting nothing but the worst from Dad. Mom said, "Prepare yourselves for when your father gets home. No one told you to play with matches." My brother Cheche and I were sitting ducks and petrified of when Dad would get home.

When Dad got in from work and smelled the fire and smoke, immediately, he asked our mom, "What happened here? And why do I smell fire and smoke?" Mom told him everything. My brother Cheche and I got the biggest beating ever, though my dad was more lenient on me since I was the younger brother. Had my mother not intervened, Dad would have sent my oldest brother Cheche to the hospital; Dad was furious. I'll tell you one thing, after that incident, my brother and I never again played with matches. We had learned a valuable lesson. It was one lesson to never again forget for the rest of our lives: *"Not to play with matches."*

The apartment in the projects only had three bedrooms, and so, all the boys slept in one room and all the girls in the other while our parents slept in their own bedroom. The buckle of dad's belt felt more like when a queen bee stung you, just a lot worse than that. Mom felt really bad for us, but she knew we had done wrong, and she knew Dad had to correct us both. Maybe Dad shouldn't have whipped us so hard, but we got what we had coming to us. My Dad didn't play, and we had to take him serious.

Nowadays, you can't even spank a child because the government wants to take them from you. I never agreed with how my dad may have punished us or treated us, but at least there was no one knocking in our doors from the government trying to remove us from our parents' home.

There were many incidents going on, but one sticks out at me and this one is about my parents. I had never told a soul and kept it a secret deep within my heart.

I was just a little boy playing with my toy cars. We had been living in Seventh Avenue projects during this time and I must have been somewhere between the ages of two through five. It was like any other day. My parents were both in the kitchen cooking, talking, and washing dishes. Dad asked Mom a question about something, but it's been too far back for me to even try to remember what it was that he asked Mom. Mom responded to his question, and since Dad didn't like her response, immediately he grabbed a rice plate from the kitchen sink with his right hand and with it, he smacked Mom across the face with it. Dad hit Mom really hard with this plate. I don't know why Dad was like that with Mom, but it sure wasn't something pleasant and a child should never have to see his or her father beat on their mother. It leaves scars that take many years for healing.

Sometime later, a young man living in our community died from a drug overdose. A few days later, his dad also died from the pain of losing his son. I was about five or six at the time. What a tragedy. This was the very first time I had ever heard about the use of drugs and about people dying. I had never seen anyone dead until this happened. Sadly, it wouldn't be the last time. Years to come, I would see some of my own friends and relatives go to the grave for the use of recreational drugs and/or alcohol. How ironic, years later, I lost some of my own siblings to drugs and my dad to alcohol. It's such a huge tragedy.

When these demonic forces creeped their way into our lives, we were not prepared spiritually to deal with them or to know what it was. We usually think that an addiction is nothing more than a person losing control of whatever substance they're on. But let me tell you, it's a lot more serious than that. There are demonic forces and powers working against these individuals, dragging them down into a world of darkness and not only against them, but even against all of us. These are the works of the devil—Satan in disguise.

-3-

ME AT SEVEN

The year is 1965 and I am seven years old. My two older brothers Cheche and Kato had all gotten guitars during the Christmas season. Since I was the youngest of the boys, I had gotten only a bunch of little toy horses and cowboy toy guns to play with. Kato, too, had gotten a set, and we both played the television program *The Lone Ranger*. We made believe that our fake toy guns were real and played shooting at each other. I also had a set of the hot cars, which were little toy cars and were very popular at the time. Gosh, how I loved those hot cars. I remember being sixteen years old, and I still had a bunch of these toy cars. We also had a set of marbles that we played with, and at times, we even played for money. I enjoy hearing music and watching my brothers as they were learning to play their guitars. When their friends Bobby and his boys came by the house (they too were musical inclined), they all grabbed their guitars and practiced playing some cool music. Brother Cheche, being the oldest of the boys, got to play and practiced with his buddies more than Kato and I. I loved watching them play. They love making jokes and enjoyed each other's company. I loved the music and the guitar playing, so I would followed them to our bedroom where they would practice, sit on the bed, and watch them practice and play their guitars. They wouldn't allow me to touch their instruments. My brother Cheche's friend Bobby played well, like if it was magic and he made the guitar sing with his fingers, metaphorically speaking. We all wanted to be like him with the guitar. Cheche was doing okay and learning whatever he could from Bobby, but Bobby was the best. As Bobby would teach my brothers the finger technique on the guitar, I watched closely, and before anyone knew it, I had become a musician. After my parents saw the potential I had with the instrument, they finally got me my own guitar and were very proud of me. My brothers knew they had a rival—me, their youngest brother. I would practice every day until I learned, and slowly I was getting the hang of things until I got good at it. It's true what they say, "Practice makes perfect." Therefore, we musicians need to practice our instruments and glorify God (Psalms 33:1-3).

Kato practiced often. He would have some difficulties at times, but he did okay. He also liked to sing. He had a good voice for singing.

Kato was also good in art and had the ability to draw well. I envy his art. He was really good at it. I couldn't compare to him when it came to art. He had talent to draw anything that came to his mind. In time, Kato would also learn fighting skills and techniques. He taught me a little kung fu some years later, but I was never like him. He was a natural and was darn good at it. He was the man, and he was a tough guy. He wasn't afraid of anybody. Due to his fighting abilities, years later, he earned his nickname, "Kato." Prior to that, my dad liked calling him Chino. His eyes were like a bit slanted when he was a young boy, but as he grew into a young teenager, he preferred to be called "Kato," and the name stuck. All his friends loved the way he fought; they enjoyed watching him as he would practice his kung fu. He was like the Puerto Rican Bruce Lee who emerged on television and in the movies. The musical talents started with us while we were all living at the CCH and Kato's kung fu fighting skills had started when we all lived as young teenagers in the Otto Kretchmer Homes

(OKH) projects, which were also known as the Dayton Street projects and were located in the south part of Newark bordering with Elizabeth, New Jersey. As you read along the pages of this book, you will learn more about the Dayton Street projects. For now, we are still living in Seventh Avenue projects.

The guitar became part of my life, and it sort of defined who I am as a person. Music is a very powerful tool that helps define people in unimaginable ways. It kept me out of many troubles. I slept with my guitar next to my bed every night for many years, and it became clear to all that the guitar and I were best friends.

While we were still living at Seventh Avenue projects, during the summer months, we all went swimming at Rotunda Community Pool, which was up the hill from us. The pool was located on the corner of Seventh Avenue adjacent to Branch Brook Park. Our oldest sister Mary was responsible for making sure that nothing happens to any one of us while our parents were out working at their jobs. There were many times that my brother Kato and I would sneak up to the pool on our own. We just loved it so much that we had a hard time staying away from it. But we all loved going swimming together and had many great times as a family.

One day, while we were at the pool with Mary, Kato decided that he was going to dive head-on into the pool. He was a good swimmer but had not noticed that he was diving right into shallow water and when he dived in, he busted his head wide open. The lifeguard immediately ran in to help him out of the water and called the ambulance while my sister turned frantic. She was worried and petrified for my brother. Kato was immediately taken to the hospital. After about two or three weeks, he was completely healed and back to his crazy self at the pool. This time around, he was being much more careful. When the incident first occurred, Mary was a mess, knowing that she was going to have to face Dad, and he wasn't going to take this very well. She wasn't too sure what she would tell Dad and kept pacing back and forth like a nervous wreck. Afterward, when we were all at home and our parents arrived from their jobs in the afternoon, all hell broke loose, but as always, Mom was able to get Dad to take it easy and calmed him down. Nevertheless, Mary still got whipped by Dad for the incident. After the whipping, Dad shouted out to her, "Next time, you watch your siblings more carefully, otherwise, it'll be worse for you the second time around."

"*Si, Papi* [Yes, Daddy]," she said. Then Dad said, "It better be the fist and last time this ever happens, you hear me?"

"*Si, Papi* [Yes, Daddy]," Mary said. It never happened again under my sister Mary's watch.

Kato and I always went to Branch Brook Park, and we loved climbing the two lion-like statues that were in the park near a lake by the park avenue entrance. Many years later, we found ourselves returning to this area of the park and reminisced about the good old days. We grew up in this park and loved going there a lot. We always wrote graffiti on the two lion statues to show that we had been there. Graffiti was inevitable for these two lion-like statues. Everyone who passed by them either wrote on them or climbed on them. It became a landmark where we would all meet if any one of us gotten lost from one another. There were so many good memories at this park. Dad loved taking Mom and the family to this park, and he loved meeting up with his friends there. Dad and his friends love drinking their beers, whiskey, and scotch at this park and goof off a bit like friends normally do. But they kept it real. No one got out of control, a least for the most part. At times, Mom may have had joined in with their drinking, but she limited herself to only a small amount of liquor. She didn't like when Dad was drinking and driving intoxicated. She wanted to make sure we all headed back home safely. Together, my parents had many good times at this park. For the most part, things never got out of control with my parents at the park, except for a few incidents when Dad would overdo it. But everybody in the metroplex loved going to Branch Brook Park.

The park had fame for the festivals it held. There were different sections of the park filled with all kinds of entertainment for everyone to play their favorite sports. It was the biggest park in New Jersey. You can see cars parked bumper to bumper one after the other as you drove around the park. Parking was always hard to find, so the people double parked their cars alongside others. Branch Brook Park circles around three cities: Newark, Belleville, and Bloomfield, New Jersey. There was a section of the park that I mostly enjoyed going to: it was Lovers' Lane. It was called Lovers' Lane due to couples going there to make out. Many years later after being married, I drove with my wife Barbie to "Lovers' Lane" and showed her where Lovers' Lane was. Nothing had really changed here, just the crowd and a new generation of people. Occasionally, some friends continued to visit this section of the park, but for the most part, everyone had moved on with their lives. During the weekends, the park had so many activities and functions that you had to get there early in order to find parking. You had your volleyball, basketball, baseball, and soccer field sections of the park and other entertainments, such as live music bands. The park had a section for horse racing, canoeing, and a food stand. Many others did barbecue. The Puerto Ricans celebrated their annual feast yearly, and everyone shared what they had. If you were single, it was the right place to meet your mate. Dad knew every inch of the park and always drove us all around the park. His favorite section of the park was the upper section, which was up the hill from the two lion-like statues. This park was always jampacked, and people from all walks of life visit with their families there. "It was well known and family oriented. Every spring season, my dad would drive the family to see the 'cherry blossom trees,' which was in the Belleville section of the park bordering with Newark." It was something we did every year, and it became a tradition. In fact, I kept this tradition with my wife while still living in New Jersey. People from different countries toured the area annually. For whatever reason, the cherry blossom trees attracted everyone to them. These tourist usually had their cameras ready to snap all sorts of lovely photos to take back home with them.

Those were the best days we ever had as a family. Whenever the ice cream trucks came by, we rushed to get in the line because everybody wanted to buy vanilla-flavored cones. They were the best vanilla ice cream cones I've ever eaten. Lines of people would form quickly, and at times, people would get back on line for a second round of ice cream cone. During my young adult years, I did lots of jogging and bicycle riding inside this park with friends and family members. This was a beautiful looking park. Indeed, God's creation is beautiful. Just breathing the air in this park brought back so many good memories.

Now back to my brother Kato in our little boy years. He was my father's favorite. Parents like to say all the time that they don't have any favorite child, but the truth is that some of them are lying, and they just don't want you to know it. I'm not saying all parents are like that, just some. Parents who have their favorites have no idea the harm this does to the rest of the tribe (other siblings in the house). Whenever Dad came home from work, the first thing he did was call out to Kato. He enjoyed playing around with him, and Kato was his favorite. Dad always had him near. He would tell jokes and make Kato laugh. It was during this time that Dad called Kato Chino. Dad didn't really show much love toward the others. When this happens, parents need to prepare themselves for what's coming. There are consequences and implications for a parent(s) that favorite's one child over another. That's a huge boo-boo!

We all addressed Dad as "sir" or "yes, sir." If he called out your name, we couldn't just say, "What?" We had to respond by saying, "Yes, Dad" or "Yes, sir." Anything other than that was considered to be disrespectful. But if anyone of us slip and responded by saying "What?" for sure we had it coming to us. That's just how Dad was, and it was part of who he was as a person. This was his rule and his law. Dad was known as Juan Del Carmen in Puerto Rico, but in the States, he was known well as Don Carmelo or Juan Carmelo, and Mom was known as Josephina in Puerto Rico and as Josefa and/or Chefa in the States. Dad was a very strict man. If we breathed around him the wrong way, we would get spanked. We couldn't even laugh at the dining room table while eating. If anyone did laugh, then that individual knew to expect getting spank. "Dad was the 'king of the castle' and everyone had to obey the king." My mom didn't have a saying in the matter. She had to go along with whatever he said. That's just the way things were at home. Dad was a bit too harsh on us, and he didn't treat Mom as the queen of the castle; she was just Mom to Dad.

Being a young boy at age nine, I remembered the Newark riots of 1967. The riots happened in the hot summer month of July 12th to July 17th (six days). My family and I were living on the corner house of Sixth Avenue and Stone Street. The Newark riots were no joke, and people were killed and hundreds were injured. The stores were being bombarded with all sorts of crimes, people breaking the windows, looting, stealing and taking whatever they can get. The National Guards were called in to assist.

Newark went through a lot of hardships during their riot days and, it took them some time to rebuild. After the riots, Newark was slowly becoming worse by the hour, but it was still home and it was where we enjoy living. My relatives loved living in Newark and we had many friends there. A few years before we had left the Seventh Avenue projects, my sister Luz took off with her boyfriend (they had ran away, eloped). Sometime later after we had moved to Sixth Avenue, my sister Luz and the guy she ran away with returned home. When they returned, they had with them their first child. It was a baby girl. She was the most beautiful and the most adorable baby we had ever seen.

Immediately, the family fell in love with her. Before their return, Dad had been extremely angry at both of them, especially at my sister's boyfriend, the baby's father. My sister was very young when she ran away from home with her boyfriend, and it made Dad furious. She was probably around fourteen or fifteen years of age when she left with him. You couldn't blame my father for being so upset at them, but the beautiful baby girl overwhelmed dad, causing him to cheer up and rejoice with both my sister and her boyfriend. Looking at his first grandchild immediately gave Dad a changed countenance. The baby brought excitement and joy to the home, causing Dad to glow. The animosity and anger that my dad felt toward my sister's boyfriend was washed away by this little child's presence. My dad forgave them both. The child turned my dad's anger into laughter and joy. Everybody was filled with joy, and the family was excited and happy. Mom too was so happy; she couldn't contain herself, and her emotions of joy were obvious to everyone.

After the first child, they had more children: two boys, and after a while, they legally married. My sister Luz was only sixteen when she legally married, so my parents signed a legal document and got them married. Luz wore a beautiful pink dress for her wedding and looked extraordinarily beautiful, stunning, and gorgeous.

Luz was mature for her age, and like any other young couple, they had their problems, but together they worked them out and pressed forward in their marriage. They lived their lives quietly and didn't bother anyone. My brother-in-law worked lots of hours on cars while my sister stayed home, taking care their three children; they were good parents to their kids. My brother-in-law made his living as an automechanic, and many times he worked under inclement weather: extreme ice-cold weather, rain, shine, snow, hot or cold—that wasn't an option for him. He worked hard and provided for my sister and his family. He didn't allow any unfortunate circumstances to get in his way; they were his family, and he took good care of them and allowed nothing to stop him. In all the years that I've known him, not once did I ever hear him complaint about his work. He knew what needed to be done and did it. My parents also visit his family periodically. We all knew each other from the projects.

Growing up in Newark in my early years was a good thing. The City of Newark was a big town and like anywhere else, there were the ghetto places and the nice places to live in, and it had everything you can possibly think of. In fact, back in the day, Newark was a great town to live in, and people from all walks of life came out to visit Newark. Some loved it so much, they stayed, and others, after returning to their perspectives towns and cities, returned to live in Newark. Businesses in Newark were growing rapidly, and the population was growing fast. We had the good, the bad, and the ugly living in Newark. Also, we had the poor and the rich people and those in between. During those days, Newark still had mobsters living in its suburbs.

After living in Seventh Avenue projects for a few years we then moved on to live in a private building located on Thomas Street, Newark. We stayed there for about a year and moved to Sixth Avenue, which was only a few blocks away from the projects. During this time I was about eight, and had built myself a shoeshine box and charged a quarter for each pair of shoes I shined. Sometimes I charged fifty cents, and at times, I got me some tips up to a dollar's worth. Shining shoes every day allowed me to make up to $25 a week. I separated a small portion and gave the rest to Mom. We lived in Sixth Avenue until I was nine, and from there, we relocated to Paterson, New Jersey.

While living on Thomas Street, my brothers Cheche, Kato, and I with some other friends were climbing up on a fire escape ladder behind one of the apartment buildings around the corner from where we lived. I was the last one climbing the fire escape, and as we're climbing up, Dad was driving by and spotted us. He immediately stopped his vehicle, parked his car, got out of the car, and approached the building, demanding we all get down immediately. As my siblings and I climbed back down, Dad started pulling our ears with a spank, got us in the car, and drove us home. Once we're home, he questioned us with, "What are you three boys doing climbing up that building's fire escape?" His question wasn't really a question but more a rhetorical statement. He then whipped us badly with his buckle belt and had us stripped naked for one week in our bedrooms. This is how he would discipline us. It was extremely embarrassing and painful, especially for my oldest brother Cheche.

Every day during dinnertime, Dad would order us to come out of the room naked. He didn't care if there was company visiting. We would come out of the room naked without wearing any clothing, not wearing any underwear, and everyone at home saw us completely naked, including the company visiting us, if any (at times there were company). Cheche already had pubic hair so you can only imagine how he felt. It was humiliating what my father put us through. This is no way to discipline a child. It causes lots of resentments, hurts, and anger against any parent. Dad would then have us kneel on our knees with a long piece of log (two-by-four) across our neck and shoulders, which we held up across our arms. He would then put grains of rice or uncooked beans on the floor and have us kneel over it, causing excruciating pain. This was the most embarrassing discipline (if that's what you want to call it) that we ever had to endure living at home with Dad. As far as I'm concerned, this isn't discipline but a parent's abuse and torture of their own children.

For Dad, it wasn't enough that we were naked, but to put a piece of log on each of our shoulders and have us kneel on rice grain and/or beans was far from discipline. He was creating monsters out of his own children without even knowing it. The pain Dad inflicted on us was internal. It's true that having grains of rice or beans under your knees while you're kneeling causes much pain, but nothing like the pains and wounds of the heart. The heart is far more valuable than any other part of the body. When inflicted, a whole knew door opens up, causing the mind to conceive nothing but hatred into your own heart from the so many hurts and pains others have inflicted on it, especially when parents are the ones that have caused the wounds. If not dealt with on a timely manner, it can cause much destruction on so many different levels. The last thing we want is a heart dictating our every move and thoughts if all it knows is pain. The heart can't be trusted: imagine when it's being torture?

My recollection is that Dad had done this to us for about thirty to forty minutes per day in the evening hours after he got in from work, once every evening, up to a week. If a parent wanted to create any animosity, anger, and/or hatred between them and their children, then this was the perfect way to do it. We were humiliated too many times. It was terrible. Since I was the youngest of the boys, I had not really grasped the severity of the matter, at least for a while. It would be some years later before I really came to grips of what really happened during those early years of my life and those of my siblings. The thought of it just spooks me out. I always knew it was wrong and that a father or a parent should never punish or discipline a child in this manner but being young back then didn't really cause any animosity between me and Dad. In my later teenage years, I did experience some of Dad's disciplines, but by this time, he had mellowed down somewhat. He had calmed down quite a bit, and his disciplinary actions weren't so bad like in past times, though some things still weren't right. The apostle Paul writes in the New Testament, "Fathers, do not exasperate your children; instead, bring them up in the training and instruction of the Lord" (Ephesians 6:4, NIV). Elsewhere, he writes, "Fathers, do not embitter your children, or they will become discouraged" (Colossians 3:21, NIV).

In other words, parents are to be careful not to provoke their children, causing them anger, resentments, and/or hatred. Parents aren't to mistreat their children, and they need to be careful how they discipline their children. Otherwise, their own children will rise up against them one day, and there will be repercussions. I'm not saying that my siblings and I rise up against our dad, but I'm sure that some of the ways my brothers treated my dad when they were older were manifestations of hurts and resentments that were held in their hearts for a long time. These are moments when parents need to sit back, meditate, and try to reflect on family values and ask themselves if they have done everything in their power to raise their children to the best of their abilities and with love and respect. I know that sometimes children do turn out to be problem children even when they are given all the love in the world from the parents, but I'm talking to those who know they have done wrong and/or to those that know that they didn't do everything right. We're not looking for perfection in our parents but love and respect. Someone we can run to when we need them. We need them to first be our parent, then our friend.

We moved to Sixth Avenue, which was only a five- to ten-minute walk to the projects, and we lived there about a year; and at age nine, my parents moved us to Paterson, New Jersey.

- 4 -

LIVING IN PATERSON

We're finally out of Newark and living in the City of Paterson, New Jersey. This was the first home my parents had ever purchased in the United States ever since leaving their home country of Puerto Rico in the early 1950s. Puerto Rico was the place of their birth and where they had been raised, but they wanted to follow the American Dream.. My parents loved everything about New Jersey.

Now that we have a new two family home in Paterson, we were all looking forward to getting acclimated, meeting new friends, and moving on with our lives. Our lives in Paterson were about to change, and we were going to embark in an unimaginable life of darkness. We lived in the north part of Paterson and quickly made many new friends both in school and in the neighborhood. Our new house had a separate garage and a restaurant next to the house. Not sure why, but my parents never opened the restaurant.

Paterson was a big city, though not as big as Newark, but it was still nice and we lived in a good area. Also, things were booming for my parents with everything falling in place accordingly. It was nice having our own home, and it sure beat living in the ghettos. Life was a bit different in Paterson, but not enough to avoid scandal, trouble, and or sorts of problems with my siblings. We all enjoyed living in our new place of residence, and whenever our parents had any free time, they loved taking us out to the park and other places for fun. Friends and relatives came out to visit from Newark and others relatives of Dad from Puerto Rico. Dad still had to commute to Newark for work. He was a hard worker and had been employed in a Newark factory for about fourteen years before he actually had to leave his job for permanent disability due to an eye injury.

Paterson seemed to be a good place for us and the people living around us and other close neighbors were nice to be around with and got along well with us. Our neighbors immediately took a liking onto us, and we all became good friends with one another. We lived on a corner house, which was a light yellowish house until Dad had the house sided with a beige aluminum siding. The neighbors on our left were Hispanics and lived in a big white house. The other neighbors on our right were a Black family and had become best friends with both me and my brother Kato. All those that came out to visit loved the house and always made nice positive comments about it. However, no one knew that the house my parents had just finished purchasing and moving into had been haunted by evil demonic forces and powers. As I mentioned at the end of chapter 2, we weren't spiritually prepared for this kind of stuff, and not to mention, we weren't ready to deal with any of it, especially because we didn't understand any of it, and much worse, we didn't know who Christ was at the time. We were from a Catholic background, went to church regularly at least once a week, but that's as far as it went, except for the fact that Mom was a devoted Catholic and did go to mass more than the rest of us. But we knew nothing of the spiritual evil world and the spirits—Satan and his demons.

None of us knew or had a clue on the journey that we were about to embark in. Living in this house and in Paterson was the true beginning of a life of turmoil, troubles, and problems for my parents and my siblings; it's where it all began to change. Prior to experiencing all the problems in this place of residence, my parents were happy to leave the chaos of Newark. It had given them a sigh of relief, but now things were about to get a lot worst. It was a new start, and it felt right for us—until the problems started at home. Mom would get up early and fix us breakfast, made sure we all dressed appropriately for school, and out the door we were. Since school was right across the street from us we would come home for lunch, and Mom would have lunch ready. Jell-O was always desert and back to school. Me, Kato, and Anne were the only ones attending grammar school across the street from us while our older siblings: Mary, Cheche, and Lulu attended John F. Kennedy High School. They took a bus to school every day, and Mom prepared them sandwiches in a lunchbox to take with them since they were too far away to come home for lunch. At times, they paid for their own lunch. I have some good memories of Paterson and all the fun my family and I had while we were living there, but when I think back, I can't help but acknowledge the evil surrounding our lives. Aside of that, Mom took great care of us and made sure that everything went as smooth as possible. We blended well in the community and made our mark. Other friends from nearby communities loved being around us as well. School was fun and exciting, and I enjoyed going to school. Unfortunately, I can't say the same about my older siblings. They love cutting class and playing hooky and attracted much trouble, except for my youngest sister Anne and I. Anne and I were like the two little saints of the house, and for the most part, we were obedient to our parents. I completed part of my third grade in Paterson all the way through fifth grade, but I didn't complete the fifth grade until I was back in Newark from Puerto Rico.

Paterson is where Satan and his evil forces schemed against my parents, me, and my siblings. Things were going so well, but slowly, it had been changing one day at a time. It was the place where my parents commenced to have real problems not only with themselves, but with my older siblings as well. I can only describe our family's troubles as "unimaginable." It seemed that trouble followed us no matter where we lived or went. My parents moved to Paterson, leaving their troubles in Newark, but trouble was only beginning and manifesting itself gradually at the very doorway of our home. In Paterson, the Vargas family would become victims of Satan. He would deceitfully work his evil deeds and crimes via my family members—my siblings—and darkness would overshadow us. It was core and within the triangle of Satan stretching all his claws into my family's hearts and minds and encircling us with darkness.

Just like it had been happening in Newark, Paterson was getting infested with all sorts of drugs and crimes, and the devil had it out for us, having no mercy, whatsoever. He inflicted my family with witchcraft, drugs, alcohol, sex, crimes, and etc.

During one occasion, my parents hired a witchcraft family and invited them to our home. When they got there, they so-called "cast out evil spirits out of the house," but what no one knew was that all they did was fill the house with more demons. My parents didn't know any better. To today, I believe that this played a big part in our livelihood. I believe that it was these demons that infiltrated our home back then that caused us to have so many problems. If only my parents had called upon the name of the Lord. But they called upon the wrong sources. Witchcraft is demonic and evil spirits take control of the person(s) calling upon them. I can't tell you how many times my siblings and I heard many strange sounds at night in the house after those people came and left our home. Some of us saw evil spirits and became spooked at night by their very presence. None of us understood any of it, but we knew it was evil. These fortune-tellers and necromancers spread water throughout the house via some kind of hand sprinkler; I'll never forget it. They asked everyone in the house to wait outside while they went in and performed some kind of ritual (witchcraft ceremonial). It was a small group of men and women performing this ritual, and one of the men, holding a hand sprinkler with his right hand, went throughout the house spreading so-called holy water. My parents had no idea what they had just done to us. Right before our very own eyes, we had just been cursed. If only my parents would have called upon the name of the Lord, the result would have been much different with positive results. No doubt my parents were ignorant on these spiritual matters and thought they were doing the family a good deed. They called in these people to come in and cleanse our home of all evil spirits, and instead, unbeknown to my parents, the complete opposite was just performed. My parents didn't understand the gravity of the situation, and by inviting them into our home, they opened the door to evil (Satan). A few weeks later, more problems and troubles followed us. In the scriptures, this is known as "necromancer," but we know it more by the word "sorcery." God condemns it throughout his word.

Many years later, after I became a Christian and given my life to Christ, God made it clear to me through the reading of scripture that all this was evil and demonic. It was sorcery and witchcraft. Satan had done a good job in deceiving my family. The more I read the scriptures, the more I became aware of the devil's masquerades. I finally understood how Satan was able to infiltrate my family's lives. He used satanic rituals via witchcraft, which is a demonic cult. The apostle Paul writes in the New Testament, "And no wonder, for Satan himself masquerades as an angel of light. It is not surprising, then, if his servants masquerade as servants of righteousness. Their end will be what their actions deserve" (2 Corinthians 11:14–15, NIV).

It was through this channel that Satan got a grip on my family and sucked his horrendous claws into our lives. His teeth sunk deep into our minds and hearts inflicting much pain and suffering. God had been trying to get our attention, but we weren't listening to his call. There were a few times that I remembered when Christians came to our homes and witnessed the gospel to my family, but my family never made a decision to surrender their lives to Christ. God calls his people time and time again, but after a while, he allows the prince of darkness (Satan) to have his way with them that reject him. I believe this was part of the problem. My parents believed there was a God, but they never wanted to make a commitment with him, and though occasionally they went to church, their lives were spiritually dead. Had they called on the Lord Jesus, he would have spared them many troublesome foes. The reading of the hand (fortune-telling) is considered evil and those that practice it have been deceived as my mother was. Aside of my parents bringing in the witchcraft mediums to the house, a recollection of appointments popped into my mind when Mom dragged me along with her to have her hand read by these necromancers. All this sorcery is very real, and the evil associated with it can be extremely dangerous. It is the same as "witchcraft." It is an abomination to the Lord, and God condemns it. He makes it very clear that we're not to engage in it. During Old Testament times, any such persons practicing such things or calling on the dead were to be put to death. God abhors it and commands us to do as well (Deuteronomy 18:10-14).

Our way of life turned out for the worse after the witchcraft ritual. My parents were having all sorts of problems with my siblings, and my siblings were doing all sorts of atrocities. It caused my parents to have more problems with each other. While living in our Paterson home, we experienced the presence of evil on a daily basis. Things were getting worse for us. Late nights during bedtime, each of us would hear a little ball dropped on the ceiling from the attic floor rolling across the attic. I didn't understand back then what all this was, but it created fear in my life and falling asleep was torture for me. My heart felt as if it were beating like about one hundred miles per hour as it pounded against my chest. This happened often—just about every night. I thanked God all that's over with, and I don't need to fear anymore. Christ is my refuge in whom I set my heart on, and he has delivered me from all these fears. Some of my siblings experienced worst experiences, but I don't think any one of them paid too much mind to what was really happening. Only at times certain noises or demonic visions would freak them out. I know for sure that my oldest sister Mary and my brother Kato had a few encounters and experiences with evil spirits to the point that it made them terrified. These evil spirits manifested themselves differently all the time via making weird noises, causing fear in our hearts. In the basement of our house, my brother Kato claimed once that he had seen an old lady smiling at him with en evil smirk. He ran steadily fast from the basement of the house to the upstairs backdoor, entering through the kitchen. I saw the look on his face, and I can tell you that I've never seen Kato scared like this before. Indeed, this demon frightened him. This happened way before his kung fu days in Newark. His heart felt as if it wanted to jump right out of his chest from the fear he experienced, causing him to turn pale. This occurred one weekday during our lunch time from school. During this time, Mary no longer attended school because she had already quit high school, and therefore, she was at home with us. Many times, Mary heard weird noises coming from the attic of the house, and she would hear as if people were walking in the attic. Also, she experienced seeing some of the same perverted demonic spirits that I experienced seeing from time to time. It occurred during bedroom hours. These demons would torment me, making me hide scared under the blanket with my head under the pillow. Sometimes, fear would grip our hearts the next day, when Mary would tell us of any unpleasant evil presence that would frightened her. She never meant for us to fear, but as she carried on to tell her story, our hearts were already jumpy. I promised that not until she reads this book, she would have not known this all these years about "causing us to fear." My other sister Lulu once claimed to have seen Satan disguised as a beautiful, handsome man. She had told us that a beautiful man had been knocking her bedroom window late one night while everyone else was sound asleep. She said the man motioned gestures with his hands—"a come-here gesture" for her to follow him, but that when she approached the window to see who it was, the man disappeared. Somehow she understood and acknowledged that it was Satan in disguise, trying to deceive her. Like Mary, she too would share with us the very next day her experiences.

I know that some of these stories may sound far-fetched to some of you, but I assure you that all these things really happened to us, and they are all true. My oldest sister Mary can testify to these events. Demonic powerful forces and their evil spirits are real and are here on earth working hard every day against every single human being in order to bring destruction to God's most precious creation—we, the people, human beings. We were created to worship God, but the devil wants us to worship him instead. I pray you choose to worship God the Father and his Son, Jesus Christ (Ephesians 6:10–18).

I like to express that it is always a good thing to pray about a house before buying it. When it comes to any and all big decisions, Barbie and I have always prayed first before buying and engaging in any business transaction. Buying a house is a big deal for us, and because of it, we always seek first God's guidance in these matters, and he has always protected us and guided us. This is important because it implicates our finances and our relationship. We have a rule in our relationship that if we have to buy any big items and one of us dislikes it, then we will not purchase the item, regardless what it is or how much we are in love with it. We must both agree on the item; because if we don't, and end up buying whatever it is, we know trouble will follow afterwards. Because of this rule in our lives, it has always saved us much grief. We've seen many couples engaged in disputes, arguments, and even fights just because they didn't make the right choices. One should only buy what's appropriate and affordable in their means of living. I promise you, life will always be a blessing for your marriage. This avoids problems in your marriages. I like to make sure my wife is happy, but it has to be within our means and not above our standard of living. Luke writes in the New Testament, "Jesus knew their thoughts and said to them: "Any kingdom divided against itself will be ruined, and a house divided against itself will fall" (Luke 11:17, NIV).

When my parents purchased the house in Paterson, neither one of them knew absolutely anything about the previous owners. In most cases, it is the norm not to really know anything about the people you're buying your residential property from. I suspect that maybe the previous owners may have been into a gothic lifestyle, though I can't say for sure, but whatever they left behind was demonic and out to get us, especially after the witchcraft rituals performed in our home by the fortune-tellers my parents hired.

I questioned Mom once about the house in Paterson and asked her to tell me what made Dad want to buy the house. She told me that the very same day she and Dad walked in with the real estate agent to see the house, the house looked as if it was sideways and crooked to her. Dad didn't see it that way. She tried talking him out of buying the house, but his heart was already set on buying it. Therefore, they purchased the home. Mom had told me that she felt an eerie spirit in the house that day. There are times when we men need to listen to our wives, and this was one occasion when Dad should have listened to Mom. This house had been haunted by demonic forces and in turn caused us lots of problems. Many years later, after we no longer lived in this house, my sister Lulu and I took a cab from Newark to Paterson to see the house one more time. We were curious. After arriving, we entered the house (though we weren't supposed to, the house was boarded by the bank), and for the first time, I can honestly tell you that the house was crooked and sideways, just as Mom had said. It was true. Our Hispanic neighbor, still living in the big white house next door, informed us that no one ever lived in it again ever since we moved out. Though the bank had the house on foreclosure, no one ever again was able to purchase the house.

About twenty years later, in the year 2001, I wanted to show Barbie where I lived as a child in Paterson, so we drove there from South Jersey and when we arrived, the house was no longer there, it was gone. I was told by a neighbor in the vicinity that the house had been burned down. Personally, I believe that God never allowed anyone else to purchase the property because it was haunted. This was the very first time in a long time that I had been there, since I was there last with my sister Lulu. We got into our vehicle, drove away, and left for good, never looking back. To this day, I have never returned. God willing, I will never again go back. God didn't want me going there anymore, and it didn't feel right being there. We are to leave the past behind us and never look back. It brought back too many sad memories that overshadowed the good ones. As I look back and I think about all the things that happened there, I thank God for always keeping me safe. No doubt his angels watched over me, and though I was still very young at the time, he did not allow the devil to destroy my life. Our God is an awesome God, and he is a great God. God is worthy of all praise and should be praised at all times. Had it not been for Jesus, who knows where I would have been today! Hallelujah!

Having the semireligious mother that I had, Mom used to pray to a bunch of statues after lighting up candles for each of the saints, i.e., statues that she had in the house on a small altar. This was Mom's "sanctuary," and it was the only peace of mind she had. The only problem with that was that instead of praying to God via Jesus, she was praying to Jesus via the "Virgin Mary," and the scriptures tell us to pray directly to God or Jesus, without another mediator (John 14:12–14; Exodus 20:3-6; Psalms 115:3-8).

God considers it idolatry even if it's done in ignorance and we are not to engage in it (1 Corinthians 10:14-22).

Satan had a grip on my family, and things were rapidly going sour for us. Within the three years that we lived in Paterson, many things went wrong and my siblings were all getting out of control except for my youngest Anne and myself. My older siblings had been experimenting with drugs and getting into all sorts of problems and trouble.

It was in Paterson that my dad started drinking heavily. He loved hanging out at the bars with his friends, and sometimes he dragged me along for the ride. Once reaching their destination, Dad and his buddies would leave me in the car, enter the bar, and spend hours drinking and amusing themselves, while naked go-go girls danced for them. During this time, Mom would be back home preparing dinner for all of us. She knew exactly what was going on but kept silent and coped with it her own way.

One day, when my siblings and I arrived home from school, we found our mom badly beaten, bruised, and with a black eye. She tried hiding it with sunglasses and makeup, but it was still visible. No one dared talking about it, but we all knew that it was Dad, and when we asked Mom what happened to her, she confessed to us that our dad had beaten her senseless. I'm not sure why Dad ever did such a thing to Mom, but the only thing I can think of was jealousy. But, folks, this is no way to treat your wife or any other woman for that matter. A man that hits or beats on his wife is nothing but a coward.

Mom was submissive to Dad's demands, succumbing to whatever he demanded. After this incident, Mom was a nervous wreck around Dad and always feared for her well-being. When Cheche saw what Dad did to Mom, it caused him to hate Dad even more so. Cheche loved Mom and hated the way Dad treated her. It turned his stomach all the time. Dad was always on Mom's case for things that were of unimportance. Maybe something was going on between Mom and another fellow and/or maybe not. But whatever the case was, Dad should have never beaten mom like that. After all, he was the father of his seven children and she was his beautiful wife. She became terrified of Dad after that incident, and her love toward Dad changed forever. I remembered how Mom always promised me that one day she was going to leave Dad when we (her children) would all reach adulthood and become independent. Nevertheless, no woman should have to put up with an abusive man, regardless of the situation. Women to men are a precious gift from God, and they are not to be handled roughly as if they were punching bags. They are given to men to be loved and cared for. They are very delicate and love to do great things for us men. God didn't give them to us so that we can abuse of them and treat them unfairly, beat them or talk down to them as if they were less than us. They are our equal and we need to treat them as such! God gave them to us as our helpers, and they need to be treated with love and respect. This incident really angered my brother Cheche, but Cheche and Dad were already having many other problems. This incident caused more tension between Dad and Cheche. This was only the beginning of things that instilled anger and resentment into my brother Cheche's heart toward Dad (1 Peter 3:7).

Besides that, Dad's drinking had been getting out of control and the fights and arguments at home were becoming a serious problem. Many times he pulled Mom by her hair, beat on her, and talked to her trashy as if she were a woman of the street, like a prostitute. My mother suffered much at the hands of my father. There were many other incidents between my parents but, some things are best left untold.

There are things in life that we should never cross the line on, and that's one of them.

My brother Cheche had the habit of sneaking out his bedroom window. Every night, he would repeatedly continue to leave the house via his bedroom window. He had some friends that didn't have any curfew restrictions, and if not, then they too were probably doing the same thing as Cheche, sneaking out their homes. After Cheche snuck out the house, he would go and meet up with his friends. I'm not sure what my brother Cheche and his friends were up to, but I'm thinking that if they were hanging out late at night while everyone in their perspective homes were asleep, then they must have been up to no good or just having a good time with the ladies. Whatever the case was, my brother was only getting into trouble. The more he stayed out, the more him and Dad had confrontations.

One night, as he attempted to sneak out, Dad snagged him and grabbed him by the throat and socked it to him (hit him). Dad had had enough. Poor Cheche, I felt so bad for him. I understood Dad for being so upset with him, but to grab him the way he did was a bad thing. Dad didn't know how to be gentle with my brother Cheche or with any one of us. Dad had a scolding temper every time he wanted to communicate with us. In fact, Dad only spoke to us whenever he had the need to question us and even then it seem like he was scolding us. Other than that, we were just his children and nothing else.

Because of what happened at home with my older siblings, many years later, Dad got really strict with me, and I paid the price for many of the things my older siblings put him through. I know that he was just trying to protect me so that I wouldn't turn out like my older siblings, but he was too strict and had a heavy hand, and hitting us for any stupidity. He didn't care what it was, and because of it, it caused my brothers and sisters to resent him more and more every day and rebelled against him. My siblings hated the way Dad treated them, especially, Cheche. Dad really had it out for him. Dad was constantly on his tail, suppressing my brother's spirit, but all that caused hatred and anger on Cheche's part toward Dad. Cheche was a well-liked guy and easy to get along with, as long as he wasn't drugged up. He was extremely handsome and had a great smile. He was able to attract you with his smile and had an Indian complexion about him, just like my sister Lulu and Mom. He had jet-black hair with a great mustache, making him stand out in a crowd. Indeed, he was a ladies' man. Something I would experience many years later on in life.

My dad was a nice man if he wasn't drunk. For being a bald man, he was very handsome. When I was still a younger teenager, I heard many women making comments about my dad about his good looks. They loved that he was handsome. Nevertheless, Dad didn't know how to deal with his problems at home. Dad suffered much grief throughout the years with my siblings. I believe that if Dad would have taken time to sit us down and talk to us with love and with a gentle spirit, maybe things may have turned out better for all of us, and the results would have been much better. Either way, it was what is was, and we all learned to live with it. The Bible instructs us clearly how parents should treat their children (Ephesians 6:4 and Colossians 3:21).

When we discipline our children, we just have to be careful to discipline them with love, sternness, and proper correction. Every parent needs to be careful when disciplining their children so that they don't cross the line and step over their boundaries (Proverbs 23:13-14).

Drinking caused Dad many heartaches. It made things so much worse, and not only for him, but for everyone at home. Maybe it was his way of forgetting his problems, who knows—only God. I believe he used his drinking as a scapegoat, but the problem with that was that he indulged and consumed his life on the bottle, overstepping his own boundaries. It caused Dad to lose self-control and for his children to dislike and reject him. We steered from his path, including Mom. Because of his strictness, I too would one day rebel against him, though not as bad as my other siblings did, but resentment and a bit of hatred settled in my heart just like it did the others. He had no easy way to reckon with. You will read about me as we move forward within the chapters.

My brother Cheche loved hanging out all the time with his friends, and he and my sister Lulu were very close to each other. Lulu was gorgeous and lovely with beautiful long dark hair and a lovely physique. She was absolutely beautiful to look upon. She had my dad's dimples and beautiful lovely legs. The guys always went bananas after her. Mom, Cheche, Lulu, and I were the darkest ones in the family, with the exception that my skin complexion is more like an olive color skin. I guess I got my complexion from both my parents. Dad's looks were more Caucasian looking like my other siblings, Mary, Luz, Kato, and Anne.

Cheche was a thief and loved stealing from others all the time. He stole from everybody and anybody he could. He stole from his own parents without hesitation and didn't care who he stole from. He stayed out late with his friends drinking, getting high, and doing all sorts of wrong things out in the streets. He did whatever he felt like doing.

While we're still in Paterson, Cheche was becoming a criminal, and for that, his life was about to change for the worst. Things were getting rough between Cheche and Dad at home. Cheche did not like Dad a bit, and dad didn't know how else to deal with him. My father's relationship with my brother Cheche's was pure hell. There's no other way to describe their relationship. Dad and Mom were feeling lost with Cheche and the pressure was mounting daily. They were desperate. Cheche was missing school a lot, and his grades were dropping dramatically, and he didn't seem to care a bit. To make things worse, Mary, Lulu, and Kato were all running into trouble, and Mom and Dad's problems continued to mount up. All of them were screwing up badly in school, skipping school and not doing their homework assignments. To add on to my parents' burdens, my eldest sister, Mary, had ran away from home.

Mary ran away from home with a guy she met from across town. He had long hair and spoke kind of funny. Sometime later, Mary got pregnant from him and had his child. This was their only child together. My parents had not seen Mary until after her son had been born. Prior to her having her child, she steered clear far from home and from Dad. When Mary returned home with her son Tony, it made Mom happy and it brought her much joy. Mom was always good to us. She was easygoing and loving. She was the one we all ran to for comfort. At times she talked really fast and loud, just like the Cubans, but she was sweet and the greatest Mom ever. Mom cooked for us almost all the time and was a great cook. Dad liked cooking, too, but didn't have much time for it, only on some of his days off. But he himself was a great chef. At home, dinner was always ready on time by 4:00 or 4:30 PM. Mom always served me an extra plate of meal caused I ate a lot. When Dad cooked for us, he would make us some serious rabbit meat or turkey meat, and boy, he can cook so good it was to die for. No one cooked the rabbit or turkey meat like my father did; he was the best chef I ever known. He cooked with wine in his meat. Everyone ate whatever he made. Indeed, he was a great cook—*delicioso* (delicious). By this time after Tony was born, Dad had cooled off with Mary and made things more pleasant for her to stay at home with us—if she so chose to (dad was upset with Mary for eloping, but now things were different). After some time, Mary did stay with us after seeing Dad's anger had subsided. Her son brought peace to my father's spirit. Dad took a liking onto him and he loved his grandson like no other. It seemed that Tony gave my dad comfort from all his problems and worries, and he became the pupil of Dad's eye. Every time Dad got home from work, the first words out of his mouth were, "Where's my grandson?" and he would call out to him. Tony was his life and joy, and Dad loved playing with him. Tony also took a liking onto my dad and loved being around him. Dad always played with him and made him giggle and laugh with his silly jokes. Tony had now become Dad's therapy. God works in mysterious ways. Who would have known that little Tony was gonna bring my dad a temporary peace of mind—only God. The author of Proverbs writes in the Old Testament, "Children's children are a crown to the aged, and parents are the pride of their children" (Proverbs 17:6, NIV).

Having our newborn nephew around the house seemed to make things better for my dad for a little while.

I like to say that I will not be the judge of my sister Mary. Only she really knows the real reasons why she left home and ran away with her son's father. Besides, I was way too young to understand her motives for leaving home. Maybe she has fallen in love or thought that she was in love with her son's father and/or maybe she could have been having too many problems with Dad at home because of his strict ways. I don't know, but sometimes, things happen for a reason. I'm not condoning my sister for eloping, let God be the judge and not me. Is so easy to condemn and accuse someone without knowing the facts. This is so ironic. When I was about eighteen years old, I had done the same. I had eloped with a girl I knew from the projects and taken her to live with me at Mary's house when she was married to her daughter's dad. The only difference was that by the time I eloped, I was already an adult, and the young girl was about a year younger than me.

During those days, before I had ran away from home, I had done it because Dad was way too strict with me, and I needed to get away from him. I needed a breather. My girlfriend and I got along great at the time, and we both agreed we can be free and do our own thing by being on our own. Had Dad not been so strict with me, I believe that I would have not had a need to go anywhere with any girl. Father was just too darn strict with me and I got tired, especially given that I was already a young adult. I felt that Dad had no right to treat me as if I were still a teenage boy. I was the youngest of the boys, and I, for the most part, gave both my parents respect. I tried very hard not to disappoint my parents. But how much of the scolding and the hitting was I going to take. In order not to raise a hand against my father (as my other brothers had done), I felt best that it was in my best interest to leave, and that's exactly what I did. Dad treated me with contempt, and I was paying for the sins of my other siblings before me. Living at home with Dad was never easy. No one really knows what goes on behind doors, only those that live in the situation. Things built up first, and one thing leads to another until you can't take it anymore. You then explode.

Sometimes, we do things without knowing the repercussions, but we do them. Whether they are good or bad, we need to learn how to adjust with the decisions we make and face reality that things will be different and learn to adjust our lives with our decisions. Otherwise, how can we balance out our lives?

LULU'S PREGNANCY

While my parents are happy with Mary's return, my sister Lulu starts acting up and involving herself with the wrong kind of men; men much older than her. This was trouble for her and things were heating up for her, especially at home. Lulu liked being Ms. Little Sneaky—too sneaky if you ask me. My sisters got along well, but Lulu couldn't be trusted. One day, it is revealed that Lulu had gotten pregnant. The only problem with that was that no one knew who the father was. The other problem was, how and what was she gonna do and what was she going to say to our parents. She was in deep over her head and didn't know what on earth she was going to do. She knew Dad would have had a field day with her if he were to discover her pregnancy. Somehow, God intervened for Lulu. God allowed Lulu to meet this new guy who kept coming around the house daily to tell her he was in love with her, though she didn't care for him, not one bit. But for the sake of everyone, Lulu became well acquainted with this young man, and she confided in him about her pregnancy and he willingly offered to help her out by marrying her and claiming the child to be his. My sister agreed and Dad accepted his proposal without ever knowing that Lulu was with child. He was a nice guy and had truly fallen for my sister Lulu and loved her. He and I got along great and so did the rest of the family. He literally saved

Lulu's life. I was young and didn't understand anything about the birds and the bees (love), but I recall the times he'd talked to me about his love for Lulu; he was crazy head-over-heels for her. For now, all Lulu's problems were over. Though Lulu wasn't in love with him, she did whatever she had to do in order to survive from the dreadful hand of my father. Lulu had pity on her new husband, but she did appreciate what he'd done for her. He was good to my sister, but problems were about to mount with them once we all left Paterson. She was only fourteen years old when she got pregnant and didn't really know much about love. After we left Paterson and went back to Newark, Lulu and her husband had many problems and finally split up, each going their separate ways. We never heard from him again.

Meanwhile, my brother Kato and I had been hanging out everywhere together with our next door friends. We played all kinds of sports, hung out in our next door neighbor's backyard, and walked many places together with other friends. We called each other silly names as we said jokes and laughed a lot. We were normal boys having fun. We loved each other a lot and looked out for one another. Kato and I had stuck together in just about everything when we were young boys. We loved playing at the Catholic school playground which was adjacent to the public school across the street from us – where we attended school together. The playground had monkey bars, rides to slide on, and a merry-go-round stand.We liked stealing little things from the sports candy store for fun; it was never anything serious. Later on in life, Kato took it to the next level and got into the habit of taking what didn't belong to him. Stealing was becoming part of who he was, just like our brother Cheche had been doing. I chose not to go that route.

DESPERATE FOR CHANGE AND LEAVING PATERSON

Dad and Mom had been feeling overwhelmed with the behaviors of my siblings, and this was causing them to have more problems with each other. Things were really getting bad. Anne and I didn't give my parents any trouble, but gradually, things had been getting out of control with our older siblings and with Dad's drinking. Everything at home was falling apart, and the pressure was mounting daily. The raising of my siblings by my parents had become nothing but burdensome. What a cross to have to carry. Satan was making his mark on my family. Dad was feeling dejected and Mom helpless. Satan had been attacking our family from all corners. Everything was just going crazy. My parents couldn't understand everything that was going on with the family. That's because it was spiritual and satanic forces had been taken over the home and the family. Satan had taken advantaged of us because he knew that we had no knowledge of God's word. He had been toying with us and taking a stand against my family. After all, my parents had opened the door to his rule when they allowed the fortune tellers to come in the house. I'm not saying that the fortune telling was the cause of all our problems, but it sure was a big part of it.

God and Jesus Christ were barely spoken of in our home while we were being raise. We didn't have any biblical knowledge of God or the devil, and the Lord wasn't a part of our lives. We were living our lives in complete darkness as if everything was all right. Satan was lurking in our home, destroying our lives and we had no clue of his schemes against us. Satan had it out for all of us and was determined to destroy everything in his path, including all of my family members, one by one. But God always has the last word. Halleluyah!

Everything at home had been spinning out of control and there was nothing but chaos. Dad was losing his patience, and Mom was a nervous wreck. Dad knew he had to do something and fast.

After much thought, they decided it was time to move out of Paterson. So after three years living in our home in Paterson, Dad moved Mom, Kato, Anne, and me to Puerto Rico and the older siblings he sent back to Newark. Cheche went to live with my sister Luz, Lulu had gone back with her husband before they had separated for good while they were living in Newark, Mary was living on her own with her son and his father but left for Newark after breaking up with him, and Luz had been married with her husband in Newark for some years now. When I returned home from Puerto Rico after five months, the family was living back in Newark. My parents gave up the house and rented an apartment at "OKH." They finally left our haunted house in Paterson for good, but the problems were only beginning to mount. It was a temporary sigh of relief for both my parents, but the reality was that it was already too late for some of my older siblings. Their hearts were already resentful and anger had set in, and there was no real changed. Demonic forces had been at work behind the scenes, i.e., the realm of the spirits.

While I was still living in Puerto Rico, Dad made arrangements to have Mom return to the States with my sister Anne. Then after another few months, he sent for Kato. When it was time for my return, Dad went to Puerto Rico and got me in person to bring me back home to the States. Before I had gone back home to the States, Dad had sent Cheche to Puerto Rico—to my uncle and aunt's house where I had been staying. I'm not too sure what my brother had done back in the States, but whatever it was, Dad needed to get him away from everything and everyone. In Puerto Rico, he still committed his crimes and did wrong. While my brother Cheche was there, he got arrested for a crime he committed that I don't dare to write about. He did prison time, and after only a few months, he was released by the Puerto Rican authorities. The authorities in Puerto Rico released him under one condition, and that stipulation was that "he would be release and put on a plane back to the States and never return to the island." Cheche was not wanted in Puerto Rico. The authorities feared he would endanger the lives around him, especially his family there. As soon as he arrived to the house from his prison cell, he packed whatever things he had and was taken directly to San Juan's airport, and on a plane back to New Jersey.. That was the last time he ever set foot on the island of Puerto Rico. Indeed he had become extremely dangerous. Not even I could believe the atrocity he had committed. I thought him better than that, but I guess I was wrong. Satan and drugs had taken a hold of his mind. Nothing fazed him, and whenever he thought to himself that he wanted to commit a crime, he went ahead and did it. He had become dangerous to society at such a young age. He was a young adult by this time. He had brought shame to the family.

While living in Puerto Rico, we stayed with my father's relatives. They cared and loved us as if we were their own children, and they had become second parents to me.

I have always wondered what my life would have been like had I stayed living there, but many years later, I acknowledged and recognized that the Lord had other plans for me. I was in his hands. Why? Because my family—my siblings and parents—were going to need me more than I could have ever imagined. Nevertheless, my love for my father's family has never changed. Forever they shall always be part of my life, and I'm grateful and thankful to God for them and for everything they've ever done for me. They are an awesome family, and I praise God for them and for the love they have always given me. I keep them close to my heart.

After returning to the States with Dad, I had to readjust to life at home. I did my best to be obedient to my parents and respected them as much as possible. Living in Dayton Street projects was not like living in Puerto Rico. Life was completely different, and for sure, I was in for some trouble. No more beautiful hot days, sunny beaches, and sitting on the balcony of the porch with my relatives. Altogether, it was a different ball game. Nothing was the same, and slowly, things started changing with me at home. Nevertheless, I wasn't a bad son to my parents. I was missing my relatives in Puerto Rico and thought of them all the time. God's plans are not like ours, and he knows what's best for all mankind (Jeremiah 29:11).

-5-

DEMONIC FORCES AT WORK

I like to start this part of the story by presenting to you the affects of how drugs and alcohol destroyed my family. In the following chapters you will read how Satan used recreational drugs and alcohol to infiltrate our home, our family and the homes of neighbors and other friends alike. Drugs were a serious problem and were slowly creeping its way into every home in the community. It was quiet and subtle, but poisonous as the snake and young people were experimenting with it, just as much as young adults were. I saw firsthand what it did to a person while living in Seventh Avenue as a child: it killed, it destroyed, it caused pain, agony, and it took away precious life created in the image of our Creator. It brings confusion, torment, and hurt to every family exposed to the enemy's tactics. It brings rivers of tears to many helpless parents; crushing their very hearts and souls, especially, to the mothers of so many sons and daughters. Mothers always hurt the most and suffer the worst pains.

It permeated its way like a plague and an unstoppable Trojan Virus. It divided my family and the families of other victims using the substance. It was a demonic curse that would follow us everywhere we went. It surged the minds of many innocent lives marking the stench of death wherever it entered, i.e., those victimized by it. Just like my parents, many of the parents living in the community or surrounding communities had not a clue on how to deal with this growing phenomenon. It would be as if one day every home would be invaded by these unseen aliens. I like to call these unseen aliens devils, unclean spirits, falling angels, and evil spirits. They are the demonic forces that exist, but we can't see them (Ephesians 6:12).

I would be thirteen years old before I would hear the word "drugs" again. It emerged, but this time around, with power and death in its grip at full force. It sprung itself into the very lives of the Vargas family—my family. It sank all its claws and teeth deep into our lives and into the lives of many relatives and friends alike. Satan knows no boundaries, and he does not respect our lives not one bit. We were bound by an environment filled with drugs, crime, alcohol, sex, guns, and Satan in the middle of it all causing havoc and chaos all around us. Satan wasn't going anywhere any time soon from the lives of my family, and neither was the abuse of alcohol and drugs. With this in mind, the Lord in his mercy would one day find his way into our lives and allow his Spirit to enter our hearts for an opportunity of a life with his Son, Jesus Christ. It was in him that we found salvation, hope, faith, and love. The question would be when, where, and how? My family and I had to first face railroads tracks of pain, heartaches, mishaps, trials and afflictions before the Lord would revealed himself to me and my siblings. Satan had us all by the throat, inflicting pain on our daily lives. The Lord allowed all these things to happen to us, due to our disobedience. We had not sought the Lord in our early years growing up when God had been trying to reach out to us. My family and I kept closing the door on God, and we paid a hard price for saying no to Jesus. We endured a hard life that could have been avoided if only we would have given God a chance and accepted Christ in our lives, way back, when the Spirit of the Lord tried so many times to reach out to us. Where there is Christ, there is love and where there is love there is God. I pray you keep an open mind as you read along and understand the objective of God's will for you, but also understand that there's a real enemy out there that we don't see with our natural eyes, but that he is as real as God is. Ignoring this concept of reality will for sure damn you one day. Heeding God's voice shall bring you close to him and guide you to the Lord Jesus's heart. Always keep in mind that "God is able."

- 6 -

RETURNING HOME FROM PUERTO RICO

I am eleven years old on a plane back home from Puerto Rico. Dad and I landed safely at Newark Airport, and from there, Dad drives us home. The only thing about the ride back home was that we weren't driving toward Paterson. We drove south from the airport about ten minutes to OKH in Newark. This community bordered with Elizabeth, New Jersey, and my parents were living on Ludlow Street, in building no. 2. OKH were a bit different than the CCH where we lived when I was much younger, but the same type of people lived in them. We had our good people and our bad people, just like anywhere else. A few months afterward, I turned twelve.

As we approached the building in the projects, Dad parks his vehicle in front of the building; we got out the car and retrieved our luggages. I asked Dad, "Why are we coming here? Who lives here?"

"We do, son," he answered.

"Oh, so we no longer live in the house in Paterson, Papa?" I asked.

"No, son, this is where we've been living ever since you left for Puerto Rico." I was flabbergasted!

As we're entering the building, I noticed the nastiness on the floors and walls inside of the building in the lobby near the elevators. There was only one elevator, and immediately, the smell of urine hovered over any good memories I may have had of living in Puerto Rico. In Puerto Rico, I had not lived this way. But here in the projects…well you can only imagine. Graffiti was everywhere: on the elevator walls, doors inside walls of the building, and the outside walls. It wasn't a pretty sight. But like everything else, when you're young and living with your parents, you try and adapt quickly to the new environment and ask no questions. It's your new place of residence and you learned how to cope and deal with things quickly and you accept how things are and make the best of everything.

We get into the elevator and ride up to the third floor. The elevator stops, we get off and off to the apartment. After a long trip, I was just so happy to be home no matter where it was. As we entered the apartment, my brother Kato was surprised to see me walk in with Dad. We hugged, greeted each other, and immediately sparked a conversation. We had lots to talk about and lots of catching up to do. Kato then says to me, "Hey, bro, welcome back home and nice to have you home."

Then I said, "Thanks, man."

He then asked, "How is it going, and how does it feel to be home?"

Then I responded and said, "I'm happy to be back, bro, it's great, but I'm a bit sad because I already miss my relatives in Puerto Rico, but I'll be fine."

I couldn't wait to see Mom, and I knew that both she and Anne would be excited to see me. I just couldn't wait to see all my family again, especially mom whom I had missed the most. I came back from Puerto Rico looking like a charcoal (dark from the sun). Playing outdoors a lot in Puerto Rico will definitely turn your complexion darker. I felt like the black sheep of the family. I was still having mixed feelings, thinking of my relatives in Puerto Rico, but once I got to see Mom, Anne, and the rest of my siblings, I acclimated quickly, and things went back to normal after a few weeks being home. After a while, my other siblings walked in, and we greeted one another with hugs and kisses. That's the norm among us Hispanics. We give each other hugs and kisses on the cheek. Everyone was happy to see me back home, and I was happy to see my family. My sister Mary was living in one of the buildings nearby in the community, Cheche was living back home, and Lulu was living by South Broad Street near the downtown area, near Lincoln Park in Newark.

Momma wasn't home yet, and I was anxious to see her. She knew I was coming home and was looking forward to my arrival. I had missed Mom and my sister Anne a whole lot since they had returned from Puerto Rico ahead of me. Sister Anne and I have always been very close and always talked about everything and anything. I thought a lot about my family while I was in Puerto Rico, and now that I was back, I was looking forward in seeing everybody. My brother Kato asked me if I wanted to go with him up on top of the building to the roof. I first hesitated but then obliged and off we went to the very top. How cool to hangout on the building's roof. It was fun to be up high above and see everything down below from a distance and everybody looked so tiny, like little ants. About forty minutes later, Mom and my younger sister Anne arrived walking toward us. As they were approaching us and getting closer, my sister Anne spots me and immediately says to Mom, "Mom, look, it's Willie. It is Willie, Mom."

They were so happy, and they hugged me immediately. It felt great to finally see them. Mom and Anne had gone up to the roof to walk down the adjacent attached building to get to our apartment because the elevator to our building was out of order. This was the normal thing to do if the elevator in your building was out of service and you didn't feel like walking up the stairs to your floor. We would instead take the elevator on the adjacent attached building to ours and take the elevator up to the eighth floor then walk up another flight of stairs up to the roof and walk across the top of the roof into our building. Once in our building, we would then walk down the stairs to our floor. It was better to do this than to have to walk up the stairs, especially if you had any grocery bags in your arms. We all went back downstairs together to the apartment then Mom cooked for us and served us a nice hot meal. Our favorite afternoon meal was white rice, red pinto beans, avocado, and two or three pieces of fried chicken. Everyone was happy and conversing.

After dinner, Mom said to me, "Ave Maria, Willie, *pero que pieto tu estas. Estas negrito y pareces que cojistes bastante sol en Puerto Rico.*" ("Oh my Willie, you are so dark. You are black and it looks like you got lots of sun in Puerto Rico.")

"*Claro que si, Mama, esclame yo! El sol en Puerto Rico siempre estas muy caliente*" ("Yeah, I know Mom, "I exclaimed."The sun in Puerto Rico is vey hot.")

Being in the sun every day changes the pigment of your skin color, and I had gotten very dark from being outdoors in Puerto Rico. I had not realized how dark I was until I had actually returned home. After a few months, my tan gradually faded, and I was back to my regular complexion, olive skin color. Afterward, mom showed me my bedroom and told me I'll be sharing it with my two older brothers, just as in the past when we all lived in Seventh Avenue projects. After some time living in Dayton Street, I found the projects to be not so different from the ones on Seventh Avenue. It may have been in a different geographical location, but everything else was the same.

The following Monday, Mom immediately enrolled me at Dayton Street School; this was the community grammar school where I completed my fifth, sixth, seventh, and eighth grade.

I quickly made friends, especially among those of my classroom and those that lived around the community. In the center of the community, there was a huge field where we played our baseball and football games. I loved playing sports, and basketball was my favorite. I'd played a good game and at times challenged those better than me. Throughout the community, I had family in both Dayton Street and Seth Boyden where my maternal grandmother was living at and some of my mom's sisters with their families. Seth Boyden projects were alongside Frelinghuysen Avenue. These were three-story buildings without an elevator. My family and relatives were spread all over these projects. We probably had the largest group of family members living throughout both communities, and we were closely knit together as one big happy family. We all had one good thing: if you mess with one of us, then you were going to have to mess with all of us. We stuck together, and we didn't allow anyone to mess with any of our relatives.

Our families' ethnicities were very mixed. We came from different backgrounds, and yet we did not treat any family member indifferent. We were family and that's all that mattered to us. Our families consisted of: Dutch, Blacks, Jews, Puerto Ricans, Whites, Italians, and etc. I think you get the picture. We were a bunch of mixed rascals and though color and/or creed may have been different from one another, we always respected each other's ethnicity. We can literally fill Madison Square Garden—that's how large of a family we were. God has a sense of humor. When he made us humans, he made us unique.

Living in the projects was not a piece of cake, but because we had so many relatives living among us, it made things much smoother for all of us. If you wanted to fit in with the crowd, then you needed to become like the rest of us. It all depended with whom you wanted to hang around with. Other than that, you were considered to be a punk, and punks got their butts kicked. Living in the projects also meant living with those of other backgrounds. Therefore, there was no room for racism. During the time I lived in the projects, the majority of the people living in them were Blacks and Puerto Ricans because the whites had been moving out to the suburbs, except for a few..

The projects were becoming dangerous to live in, but for us that lived in them, fear was not a factor. You had to know who your friends were and who wasn't. That's just the way it was, and everyone knew to always look behind their shoulders. This was our way of life, and something we all had to get used to. Either you adopt quickly or you move out and move on with your life. Living in the projects taught me to pick and choose my friends. Otherwise, I could have easily found myself doing the wrong things with the wrong people. I'm not saying that I was some kind of saint, but in order to survive, we had to be careful. Trouble was always lurking everywhere. Those of us who lived in the projects quickly became street-wise, and had great friends whom we can trust. Not everyone was a friend, but for the most part, everybody knew each other living in the community.

Unfortunately, living in the projects is also a community where the use of recreational drugs and alcohol is a huge problem. Because of it, my family members, relatives and friends alike, lost their lives. Fighting was essential for many of us if we wanted to survive. Some were bullied around and others fought back. I wasn't a fighter. I had my friends who were like me and stayed out of trouble as I did. Maybe because I had older brothers others didn't mess with me. I rarely got into trouble or in any fights. But living in these buildings made us fearless, though we still had to look out for our own backs and be aware of our surroundings.

My brother Cheche was a good fighter and boxed well, but Kato was skilled in martial arts while I was just a young, quiet teenager. Kato devoted much time to his fighting skills while I was more of a socialist, and Cheche was in his own world of drugs. Kato used drugs daily as well and I learned only but a bit of kung fu from Kato. It came in handy when I most needed it, but nothing to brag about. For sure I couldn't compare it to Kato's. Kato wasn't someone you wanted to stir up any trouble with. He had too much of a fighting fever and did not hesitate to quickly put anyone in their proper place. Once in a while, Kato would have to fight somebody, but for the most part, everyone respected him.

I got jumped a few times living in the projects, but with the little kung fu I learned from Kato, I fought right back and never showed any fear. Showing fear would have only cost more problems for me. I thank God I never got into anything serious. His love has always watched over me. Now I know Jesus, so I don't fight anymore. I let God fight my battles. He's stronger than my enemies and much stronger than me. There were a few other incidents after that, but nothing to brag about. Living in the projects made us tough and alert all the time.

My older sisters were cool girls and were doing their own things. Mary had her own apartment in building six and my sister Lulu was still living off of Broad Street for a while with her boyfriend until they moved in with our parents for a while until they were able to get their own apartment (this was before Lulu's second daughter was born). She had lots of friends but had been dealing dope with her daughter's father for a living. But Lulu was a very nice young lady, easy to get along with, and everyone loved her. She was beautiful looking and she had the most adorable dimples and was never conceited.

LULU AT DAYTON PROJECTS

While Lulu was staying home with her boyfriend, her boyfriend and my dad had a sharp confrontation. Lulu's boyfriend wasn't working and was idling around the house in their bedroom doing nothing but sleeping and watching television. He was freeloading at home while dealing dope, and my dad got suspicious and hipped to what he was doing, so Dad demanded they leave and get their own place immediately. I was home when this incident occurred. I felt bad for Lulu and so did my parents, but given the situation, it was best for them to leave. Had my brothers walked in on a time like this, all hell would have broken loose, and who knows what would have happened at home that day. Immediately after their confrontation, Lulu and her boyfriend packed their personal belongings and left the apartment.

Sometime shortly after the incident, the Newark Housing Authority approved for them to have their own apartment in building five; it was in the same community we lived in.

Lulu and her boyfriend both made a living by dealing dope, and neither one of them held any jobs. Shortly after they had gotten their own place, she was found with child and gave birth to another daughter. Not too long after living in their own apartment, he went to prison for possession of drugs. Someone tip the cops off and raided their apartment while Lulu was elsewhere. If my memory serves me right, he had been sentenced to serve five years behind bars in a state penitentiary prison.

It was hard for my sister Lulu seeing her man incarcerated, but there was nothing else she can do. There's an old saying, "You do the crime, you pay the time." Nothing good comes out of dealing dope. Many have taken this life to make easy money, but at the end, either they end up dead or behind bars somewhere. This kind of life never brings peace, and those indulged in it have to always look behind their backs. It brings nothing but problems and endangers not only your lives, but the lives of your love ones and those involved. According to God's word, all these things fall under sorcery and rebellion against God. The apostle Paul touches on some of these things in the New Testament and makes it very clear to us. He also writes a bit about the things that will get us into the very throne of God. It's all up to us to choose (Galatians 5:16-26).

BRANCH BROOK PARK FESTIVITIES

Meanwhile, an event of the biggest annual festivities was coming up at: "Branch Brook Park Festivities," which was located in Newark. This was during our first years living at Dayton Street projects, and it was during the summer month festivities of September 1, 1974. My family and I went to the Branch Brook Park festivities as we did annually for the biggest festival of them all. Everything was going well. Music was playing and people were enjoying themselves, having the time of their lives. It didn't matter which way you try walking through, the park was extremely crowded with people from all walks of life. Every Hispanic resident living in Newark and the metroplex areas were there. One can hear the sounds of joy from one end of the park to the other. Everything was going well, i.e., until all hell broke loose.

It was during the Puerto Rican Day annual festival. That day in particular, the park had been packed with thousands of people who came out to enjoy the festivities. People from New York, Connecticut, Rhode Island, and of course, New Jersey had been there having a good old time. For entertainment, the festivities had a grease monkey tree in which any volunteers would climb the tree for a big price. The person(s) climbing the tree had to make it all the way up the tree in order to win the price, but if they didn't make it all the way up, then they would be disqualified to climb a second time. There were food stand vendors everywhere in the park with Puerto Rican musicians playing loud Latin salsa music, and there were games of all sorts to play. During the course of the festivities some participants were being observed breaking the law, each of which was a violation of Essex County Park's regulations, and all hell broke out. I was there with my family when this incident occurred, and I was sixteen years old at the time.

After all hell broke loose, people ran confused from one direction to another, not knowing where they were going. This incident caused a riot to break out. Everybody at the park got disoriented as we all ran for cover. Nobody wanted to be victimized in any way possible. Other fights broke out, and things only worsen. There was chaos all over the park, and the authorities were called in. I don't remember if the National Guards were also called in to try and keep the peace and things under control, but the Park police couldn't handle such large crowds.

Fun suddenly turned into danger. The musicians on stage stepped down and ran for cover after they saw that the people were throwing rocks and bottles at the police. I think that everybody was confused that day. It was such a crazy event. I remembered clearly seeing many people running toward their vehicles in shock of what had just occurred at Branch Brook Park. Prior to this incident, I had never seen chaos in any festival of this magnitude. My parents split up from us, so we all had to find our own way back home. By the time I reached home, everyone had been there safe and sound. Like my dad, I too knew every inch of the park, and that day, it served for my well being. I admit that it took me a few hours to get home, but I got there safe and sound, and that's all that mattered to me and my family. I just thank God that none of us were hurt. There were other relatives there, and they too were fortunate enough to get out uninjured. Others weren't so lucky. It was such a horrible situation. Some people were hurt with blood running down their faces. I don't remember if there were any casualties? All I knew was that my heart was pounding hard, and I needed to get out of there as soon as possible. The Park police themselves were scared of the crowds and quickly backed off when Newark Police reinforcements arrived at the scene and took control of the situation. There were bottles flying everywhere and all around us. Fire bottles were being thrown at the police vehicles, other vehicles were being flipped, and the riot pressed on for a few hours before things were finally in the authorities' hands. What a scary place to be in at a time like this. All chaos had broken loose, and Satan had instigated the entire riot. I like to call it like it is.

Satan knew exactly where and how to attack. Everything had gotten way out of control. Prior to the event, everyone was having a great time. People were laughing, drinking beer, playing games, dancing, and having all sorts of fun. Unfortunately, many were high on dope (drugs) before they got to the festival. Others had been getting high at the park with the use of marijuana and cocaine while others got high on popping pills (swallowing pills). People were drinking all over the place.

After that incident, neither I nor my family ever went back to another festival at Branch Brook Park. I am not sure if the City of Newark had stopped the annual festivals held at this park, but I do know that after this incident occur in Newark's Branch Brook Park, the days that followed were under tense situations because of the many crowds that went to the streets, and pressured mounted, while the Mayor marched to City Hall with a contingent from the crowd and police escort in hopes of diffusing the situation which was only getting worse by the hour. Fires were reported throughout the City of Newark and some incendiaries were reported during the Labor Day weekend, and I believe it may have gone for another few days in September 1974, before it all came to a halt, but not without extensive damaged to the City of Newark. In fact, many businesses were threatened by the many crowds, and this incident altogether costs the City of Newark lots of money. Branch Brook Park was a great park, and because of this riot, it hampered many other activities. It really was the best park in all of New Jersey.

DEATH OF LULU'S BOYFRIEND

Shortly after this incident my sister Lulu's boyfriend still a few years into prison, was diagnosed with a disease that claimed his life, so he never got to complete his full sentence behind bars. His family and ours all went to his wake and funeral. At his funeral, my sister Lulu met a relative of his, and after some time went by, Lulu got involved with his relative—one of his uncles. He was good to my sister, but unfortunately, he was a bigger drug dealer than his nephew; he was a mobster, and big time drug dealer.

Lulu was deep in over her head. Getting involved with a mob drug dealer was no joke and nothing to take lightly. I admit that he really was good to my sister, but like any other mobster, he had many enemies. He was a gentlemen and always very cordial with the family. When things seemed to be booming for my sister and her new guy, out of nowhere, some men came up to him one night and shot him dead with a double-barreled shotgun at close range. He was killed right near his hotel room building where he lived on Broad Street.

- 7 -

CHECHE AT DAYTON PROJECTS

Meanwhile, my brother Cheche is still out in the streets committing all kinds of crimes and committing or sorts of atrocities. He's completely out of control and stealing from everybody and anyone. He had been robbing people and holding them up with guns. He broke into many houses and took whatever valuables he can find. He put many lives in danger, stealing from them their most valuable possessions and their money. This was his daily living.

Cheche was dangerous to himself and to society, but because he did all this just to get a fix—drugs—he did not care a bit who he hurt or endanger. He had become a big time junkie (drug addict). Many people were starting to fear being around him. At times, he committed some of his crimes with some of his closest friends. They were doing the same things, and they didn't care who they hurt or committed their crimes against. As long as they got what they wanted, that's all that mattered to them. Whatever was of value, they went for and sold to others, got their money, and spent it all on shooting dope into their arms. People were afraid of them. No one wanted to accuse them, afraid of what would happen to them once the authorities would release them from prison. Everyone in the community knew about the things they had been doing, but everybody turned a blind eye to it. Cheche had been constantly doing this sort of thing in order to keep up with his drug addiction. Many people don't understand that this is a very expensive habit. Every addicted junkie on heroin will tell you the same. To maintain your drug addiction, you need as much money as there is grass in a field; that's how bad it really is. Cheche was stealing from my parents and from everybody else. He spent his life in and out of jail. Being out of prison was as if he were on vacation for two or three months and then back in. It's like he had become immune to prison and it didn't faze him anymore. What a way to live. It's true that my parents weren't perfect and Dad was very strict, but this they did not deserve. After all, Dad only wanted what was best for us. Maybe Dad didn't know how to express how he felt for us, but at the end of the day, he was still Dad and provided for all of us. Cheche really pushed Dad's buttons, and unfortunately, it was too late for Dad to try and show Cheche that he cared for him. They had no kind of relationship, and Cheche was beyond that. I believe that if Dad would have gotten in Cheche's way, there may have been the possibility of Cheche going hey-wired on Dad to the point of either hurting Dad or even killing him. Cheche feared nothing and didn't get along with Dad. Cheche had been consuming drugs all day and night.

Satan had his grip on my brother Cheche, and now it was a lot worse than ever before. If you looked at his arms, he had needle tracks up and down his veins. It was horrible. He was doing so much drugs that he started poking other parts of his body to get high.

Addiction to drugs is an addiction of death. There's no life, and everything you do, you do it to support this horrible habit. All you do is shoot dope all day long and live an extremely dangerous life. Without God, we're lost in this sinful world, and we're just walking zombies: alive but spiritually dead without any hope, direction, and far fetch from the truth of God's righteousness, without Christ and an abundant of life (1 John 4:16–18)..

We were created to worship God through Christ, and in him we have excitement, joy, and love. God gives us the things we really need, and in him we have fulfillments, dreams, goals, and accomplishments. Living a life of drugs is a life of shattered dreams—dreams and images of dark shadows that haunt our lives daily and brings us down to nothing, stealing our identities and any form of hope. It's a life of destruction and confusion until it finally takes us down to our own graves.

It was sad to see how Cheche consumed and destroyed his life away by his use of recreational drugs. He was no longer the same brother I knew. His mind was gone to a place of darkness and only God was his only hope for any survival. Cheche had become one of Dayton Street's most dangerous dope fins, him and a few others with him. My parents had many sleepless nights because of the things he had been doing, him and my other siblings.

Cheche spent many nights out until the early morning hours. He never looked good, i.e., he was always high on drugs. His presence at home was disturbing, scary, and frightening. He was still our family and we still loved him unconditionally. Many times, Mom would try and talk some sense into him, and he would nod his head acknowledging Mom, but to no avail. There were times he went into the bathroom and not come out until about forty minutes later, holding a syringe in his hand. This meant that he was shooting another dose of dope into his veins as his drug affect from his previous high was wearing off. That's how bad his drug habit was. He had to be drugged at all times in order to function, if that's what you call functioning. He didn't care if we saw him holding the syringe (needed to shoot dope into his arms) in his hand. This was so painful for my parents to see. He broke their hearts and my parents were helpless and at a loss, not knowing what to do with him or how to help him; they had ran out of options.

God was the only one that would have helped him, but God was nowhere to be found because my family and I hadn't been walking with the Lord during these times. God would have protected us if only we would have known him. My parents and I didn't read the Bible. It's true that we went to church mass once or twice throughout the year, but that was as far as it went. We didn't fear God because we didn't really know him (Psalms 25:12–15).

Cheche was lost to an evil world of pure darkness, and his life had changed dramatically. Somewhere along his path, he had taken a wrong turn and couldn't find his way back to break away from it. Satan had him bound for hell to a life of crime and depravity. He didn't mean to do the things he did. But the powers of darkness controlled his every move. Demons possessed his body and took over. He just couldn't help himself anymore. Drugs had taken full control of his life, and Satan didn't allow Cheche to seek the proper help he really needed to be set free from the demonic powers that had taken control of his life. If at any time he tried to change, Satan would keep pulling him backward to a terrible life of drugs and crimes.

It was countless times the many times my family and I went to visit him behind bars. When he wasn't under the influence of drugs, he was such a nice guy to want to be around with. In jail, he was always with good behavior, though at times he was provoked by other inmates and had to fend for his life on different occasions. At times, jail can be worst for some inmates than being free out in the world. My heart always went out to him. I always knew deep within my heart that the things he done were only done because of his drug addiction. He promised always that whenever he get out of jail, he would be a different man, but every time he came out, he would only returned to doing the same things over again. In fact, he would get worst. Every time he was released out of prison, after about a week, he was back to his old self. It's like an alcoholic when they are addicted to their liquor. They are bound to it and no matter how many times you hide the bottle from them, they'll find another way to get another. Well those addicted to drugs are the same way, but worst off because of the horrendous crimes they commit, just for a fix. They need our prayers for God's deliverance.

Unfortunately, the more Cheche indulge in drugs, the worse he became, making each situation worse. It was a constant battle for my parents to have to deal with my brother. Cheche was causing them much heartaches, pains, and tears. No one knows the sufferings parents go through with their children at home unless they themselves experience the same kind of things with their own children. That's why no one should judge without knowing the facts. Instead, we should be careful to pray for those that are going through rough times with their children and if possible, give them a helping hand. We should learn to ask God to intervene for them. God can take one good deed that we do and turn it around to make someone's life better. There are so many people victimized by the use of drugs, prostitution, and alcohol, that unless we stretch our hands to them, many may never make it and may be lost for all eternity (Isaiah 57:2). Personally, I have seen how God has delivered many of these souls from the strongholds of Satan, but in order for that to happen we must witness God's love to them with our actions. God loves repented sinners, and when the Holy Spirit touches them, I promise you that everything changes (Ezekiel 18:21–23).

It is vital that parents seek God and instruct their children to do the same. When parents aren't willing to go the extra mile, they are risking their own children for disaster. Many young adults have lost their souls to hell because no one ever extended a helping hand when they needed it. I pray that's not one of us. At least my parents tried to do something to help my siblings. Maybe they didn't do everything they should have, but at least they did whatever they could. This is why it's so important to raise children in the ways of the Lord. Perhaps, some of my siblings who are deceased today may have still been alive if we would have known the Lord according to the scriptures. Sadly, we didn't know God the way it's written about him in the Bible.

Many red flags had been raised while we lived in the ghettos, but no one really paid any attention to them. The terror of drugs surrounded our community, spreading its feathers throughout almost every home. Many parents living in the community were aware of the drug problem, and many knew that their own children were using it, but because they didn't know what to do or how to handle the situation, they turned a blind eye to it. No one really wanted to talk about it or addressed the situation. It was sad to see how many of my friends and relatives, including my own siblings, fell victims to Satan's trap. There were so many good families living in the projects, and yet no one knew how to counterattack this epidemic. Drugs echoed a buzz of death into the hearts and minds of every soul that Satan struck with his demonic claws. Satan was victimizing the whole community by keeping his demonic forces in place. Drugs claimed the souls of many of our love ones. This is why every family should seek God while they still can before is too late.

-8-

MY SISTER LUZ IS PRONOUNCED "DEAD"

On April 5, 1971, approximately fifteen days before my twelfth birthday, Luz was pronounced dead at martland hospital in Newark, New Jersey (almost four months short of her nineteenth birthday). She was the very first sibling who went home to be with the Lord. According to Luz's death certificate the cause of death was due to cardio respiratory arrest intracerebral hemorrhage. She died in the operating room while her doctors were performing surgery on her. This was the same hospital where all my siblings and I had been born except for my two oldest sisters: Mary and Luz: they were born in Puerto Rico. Many years later, I heard that the City of Newark built university hospital in place of martland hospital and made the old martland hospital a place for the elderly and those impaired with mental and other disabilities.

When my sister Luz died, it devastated my family and tore my mother apart. I remembered it vividly. Luz had been sick for some time now in the hospital, and my parents went to see her every day. My parents were optimistic and hoping for a miracle. When she died, it sent shock waves throughout the family and friends alike. No one was expecting for her to die on us. This was a tragic moment for my parents and family and drained my mother sick for a long time. It pierced her heart. This happened after a few months after Dad and I returned from Puerto Rico. Luz was well loved by my parents and by all of us, her siblings. She was well loved by everyone and had many friends in New Jersey and New York City. Her husband's family in New York loved her as well. Her husband loved her so much that after she passed on, he vowed never again to legally marry, and so, he kept his promise. Mom took it the hardest. Luz was such an amazing young lady. She had three children by the time she reached her eighteenth birthday. They were her life, and she loved them and took great care of them. She was funny, witty, smart, intelligent, and sociable. After her death, her children were raised by their father and his family. At the funeral home, the wake was immensely crowded with family and friends from across the northeast. I was in complete awe when seeing the amount of people that attended her wake. Many came out to pay their respects and peoples' hearts were touched by the loss of my sister. My uncles living nearby gave my parents much support. I will always be grateful to them for being there for my parents. Had they not been around at the time and gave Mom the support she needed, I don't think she would have ever made it. Her pain was unbearable, and it devastated her to the point that her doctor kept her under medication to help her cope with her loss. The medication sort of kept her a bit sedated; they were tranquilizers. Mom was such a mess during those days. She wore nothing but black clothing for a very long time. I think she wanted to keep my sister's memory alive as much as she could, but this only affected her even more, and it caused her nothing but pain and suffering. To this day, I have never seen Mom cried and suffered the way she did for my sister Luz.

At the wake, as I approached my sister's coffin and saw her corpse lying there, it really tore into me. I tried holding back, but a knot formed in my throat and I could not stop weeping. The pain in my heart was too deep and bigger than me. In fact, ever since Luz died, I've never remembered ever weeping for anyone else like that, not even for my other siblings who died years after Luz. There're things in life that we just can't explain. I was only eleven going on twelve when she died. It was hard seeing my sister in her coffin, and everyone was in disbelief. My sister Luz's death sent a sharp dagger right through my heart, ripping it apart into tiny little pieces. After her death, the doctors at the hospital handed Mom my sister's hair, and for many years, Mom saved it in a yellow envelope locked away in a small safe box, which she kept in a luggage. Occasionally, she'd retrieve the envelope and reminisced about my sister Luz. She loved talking about her, but it always saddened her, causing her to shed many tears, and only made her suffered. It was always hard to see Mom like this, but I always gave her a shoulder to lean on, metaphorically speaking and a lending ear to vent on. This went on for many years, and after about another ten or fifteen years had gone by, I never again heard mom speak about the matter ever again.

After the wake and the funeral service was over, family and friends gathered together for the nine day religious ritual (the rosary prayer), and anyone wanting to participate came out to the house and joined the religious prayer. After the rosary prayer, coffee was served with Ritz Crackers and cheese. The rosary lasted for about two or three hours per night. The rosary prayers lasted for nine days. This is the normal thing to do among Hispanic Catholic families after the death of their love one(s).

One night after the rosary and after everyone had gone to their homes, my oldest brother Cheche came in from outdoors all drugged up and almost dropping dead on the floor from an overdose. He had taken a bunch of pills and gotten an overdose from them. We all got scared and feared for him. It was devastating, one blow after the other. My parents and an uncle kept trying to keep him awake, tapping him on his face with a wet towel, wiping his face and Mom putting her fingers down his throat until he was able to vomit the pills out. They were able to keep him awake, and immediately after vomiting the pills, he was rushed to the nearest hospital. It seemed that he tried committing suicide, but God was merciful and didn't allow him to die. Cheche was very close to our sister Luz, and her death affected him big time. When my parents asked him why he drank the pills, he responded by saying that he couldn't live without his sister, Luz, and that he was missing her a lot. Cheche spend lots of nights at my sister's house with her and her husband and had become really close to them. But with this blow, he had a hard time dealing with it, and it really tore him apart.

Luz loved Cheche a lot and got along well with him. I'm not sure that my parents had really grasped the severity of their problems with my brother, but as long as they knew he was staying with my sister Luz, they didn't push to remedy the problem. This was just the beginning of my parents' problems with Cheche, and little did they know that one day, he would literally put them through hell on earth. Everything was rapidly changing, things were getting worse and my parents already had their hands full, with their own marital problems.

As I mentioned earlier at the beginning of this chapter, my sister Luz was the first one in our immediately family to make it to heaven. I was told that a pastor from a local church in Newark had gone up to see her at the hospital, prayed for her, and led her in prayer to the Lord; she received her salvation in Christ, and I'm confident that she's now with the Lord in his presence. Praise God!

A few times when we were young, I remembered Christian families visiting our home and sharing the gospel with my family. They always prayed and spoke to my parents about Jesus. I was way too young so I didn't understand any of it. The only thing I can say is that God had been trying to get my parents' attention for a long time, but no one at home was really listening. By his grace, love, and mercy, my sister Luz made it to heaven. Thank God for Jesus, because though my parents didn't know God, they had some friends or knew of Pentecostals that knew the Lord and they were the ones that went and prayed for my sister Luz at the hospital. God was trying to spare us from the enemy (Satan) and from a life of suffering, pains, and hardships. Maybe Satan knew all along that the Lord had chosen my family for salvation, but because we were blind to God and hard of hearing to his word, Satan took advantage of our situation and infested our lives with sin. He did everything in his demonic power to keep us far from God and from his Son Jesus (James 4:7–10).

Dad took to alcohol and Mom followed after a few years. They could have done much better. Hanging with friends that drink all the time is what we end up doing after a while and our lives are changed and darkened for death and the grave unless we get help before it's too late (Psalm 23:4).

Losing my sister Luz at such a young age had taken its toll on my parents, and the fact that they were having so many problems with themselves and with my older siblings only made things worse, and with Satan lurking in our lives, we had no chance for redemption; he blinded our minds (2 Corinthians 4:4). By this time, darkness overshadowed any light that Christ may have been sending our way.

> Then Jesus said to them, "Don't you understand this parable? How then will you understand any parable? The farmer sows the word. Some people are like seed along the path, where the word is sown. As soon as they hear it, Satan comes and takes away the word that was sown in them.
>
> Mark 4:13–15 (NIV)

-9-

KATO FOLLOWS AFTER CHECHE'S FOOTSTEPS

Meanwhile, Kato was out of control, staying out all hours of the night, and my parents were feeling lost. It didn't help much that by this time, both my parents turned to booze (liquor) and every day they were consuming booze as if it were water. Can you imagine? Now we had both parents indulging in alcohol, and instead of finding solutions to their problems, they only added to it. I guess it was the only way they knew how to deal with their problems. Seeking professional help didn't occur to them. It already seemed to them that no one had the answers to their problems, so drinking became their comfort zone, and it was their scapegoat in dealing with their problems. We need to equip ourselves with the right tools, engage head on, and work at them gradually with the guidance of the Lord.

Kato became a huge problem just like the others. He's on a path following my brother Cheche's footsteps and liked hanging around with the wrong people, though not at all times. He allowed himself to be influenced by them and enjoyed using recreational drugs just as Cheche and my two other sisters: Mary and Lulu. He was a very handsome young man with a well-structured physique. After sometime past, he increased the amount of drugs he was using and continued getting high on drugs with his friends. Just like Cheche had done many times before, Kato had been coming in from outdoors late at night, really high on his dope. When a drug user becomes an addict, he or she is considered a junkie, and once they get to that level, they be so high and out of it, that they start scratching their chin or face and/or any other part of their bodies, especially their arms. They cannot help themselves at this point. The demonic hold that Satan has on them is way too powerful, and unless the God of heaven sends his Holy Spirit to deliver them, they then end up getting worse as each day passes by. Cheche did these same things.

My brothers had become extremely dangerous to my parents and to others. For this very reason, me being the youngest of the boys, it gave me an advantage to observe, and it helped me to choose my friends. Although I was no angel, I too did some things that I should have never done, and I'm sure not proud of any of it. I actually learned from those mistakes. Had Jesus not come knocking on my door when he did, I would have probably ended up just like my siblings. No one is exempt. That's why we really need to be wise and careful with whom we allowed to befriend us. The apostle Paul in the New Testament writes, "Do not be misled: "Bad company corrupts good character" (1 Corinthians 15:33, NIV).

Personally, some of the guys that my brother Kato hung with weren't the type of guys one would really want to be around with. I didn't like some of them. I can smell a dirty rat from far away, and whenever Kato brought any of them home, (my parents apartment), I kept alert, knowing and limiting my conversations with them. They just weren't the kind of guys one would trust in. They were trouble, and I was hipped to their ways. I didn't trust and of them. I hated when these young men came to visit with Kato. A quick glance at their eyes and I can see the evil in them. After a while, a person can discern the evil from certain kind of people that have nothing good to offer. Good thing they didn't try to mess with me. They knew my brothers Kato and Cheche weren't going to have it, and neither was I, and my brothers weren't a force to reckon with. Whatever my brothers said, they knew to go along with. These men supply Kato with drugs, and they did many other things that just weren't right.

Things were rapidly changing, and we were growing up fast and streetwise. Living in the ghettos, one must quickly learn to catch on quickly. That isn't too much of an option. If you want to fit in and survive, then you must wise up and follow the flow of things. At least that's how we thought back then. By this time, Kato had it with school and decided to drop out, and there was absolutely nothing my parents could do. He was giving Dad a heck of a time. My dad tried talking to him about the things he was doing and about how he was throwing his life away and hanging out with the wrong people and using drugs, but as Dad was lecturing my brother, Dad suddenly got so furious with Kato, he lashed out on him to hit him, but Kato lashed right back at Dad. Dad tried to grab him to hit him, but Kato got up quickly from the kitchenette chair and blocked my father from hitting him with the chair. It was horrible. My mom was finally able to get in between to stop them from fighting, and had she not done so, for sure my brother may have hurt my father. Kato was already a darn good martial arts fighter by this time, and he wasn't going to allow Dad to lay a hand on him. Many parents don't understand that when a son or daughter is under the influence of drugs, they just can't charge at them or attack them that way. Though, I don't recall my brother being drugged up that day. My recollection was that he was sobered, but Dad nagged on him and tried hitting him. I'm not saying that Kato had a right to do what he did, of course not. But Dad didn't understand the magnitude of the situation so he reacted toward my brother with anger. Now, if my memory serves me right, Dad was a bit woozy on booze and had a little too much to drink that day. That only added to the problem. Parents really need to reach out to their children with love. If that doesn't work, then maybe they should try and find their children the professional help they need. It's not about calling the authorities on them and putting them behind bars. This is okay if they commit crimes that make them dangerous to society (though Cheche was dangerous to society by this time), but Kato was still smart enough to know better, even though he loved using the substance. Counseling from church leadership may also help if the church is equipped with such ministries and the child is willing to participate in any sessions. Parents should also go to church regularly (Mom still went, but not as much).

The minds of addictive addicts are controlled by Satan, and he doesn't allow them to think straight. Though Kato still wasn't so bad yet, he was using quite a bit of drugs daily. He was Dad's favorite and now he has become Dad's enemy. How sad. It was such a tragic to see my family going astray. Christ loves us all the same. He doesn't favor one more than the other. Because of his love and his death for humanity, salvation is equally distributed to all mankind without partiality (1 Timothy 5:21 and John 3:14–21).

At this point, Dad demanded Kato to leave and live anywhere other than home. I felt bad for both of them. Father and son fist fighting each other? Kato crossed the line. I understood Dad's frustration. Just that he went about it the wrong way. All he wanted was for his son to have a better future. No one could blame Dad for being so upset at Kato. He was extremely disappointed with him. Dad may have been too strict with us, but I know deep inside my heart that he meant well. For that, no father should be blame for wanting to correct a son and/or daughter. It's true that his strictness was to the extreme, but he was still a father trying to keep chaos under control and at the same time still provided for his family. He still loved Kato much, but Kato couldn't see it. Kato was in his own little world, and Satan had him blinded to his father's correction. Dad had it with all the junk that was going on with his children. He was under a lot of pressure. I look back and can honestly tell you, I don't know how he survived as long as he did with all the nonsense my siblings put him through.

No parent deserves what my siblings put my parents through. Our job as grownups should be to repay them with good when they are too old to look after themselves. Drugs and alcohol are serious problems for many families across America. It's true that our country has many different programs that can help alcoholic victims and drug addicts, but many families wait too long to take any action in getting the proper help they need. Many wait until is too late. Parents don't understand the world of drugs unless they themselves have experienced that kind of lifestyle. Many parents need to get better educated in order to deal with these kinds of problems more effectively. And they should take care not to mistreat their children because in doing so, sooner or later, they will strike back, and there are serious repercussions.

By this time, drugs had been consuming Cheche, Lulu, Kato, and Mary, though by this time Mary was married, and living on her own with her new husband. She too had been messing around with drugs, and this was causing her serious marriage problems. It was consuming her marriage. My youngest sister Anne and I were the only two who were obeying our parents and showing them some respect. Though, I admit that at times, I wasn't at my best behavior; I did little sneaky things. Though none of us were fond of our father (he was rough with me and Anne), I still loved him and respected him. It would kill me to disrespect him. Whenever Dad scolded me (he did plenty of that), I would immediately put my head down and not answer him a word. I would not dare to look at him. It was my way to show him some respect, though he always got upset at me for doing that all the time. I would be petrified to disrespect him. Not because I was afraid of him because that wasn't the case, but because he was my father and I knew better. He had been disrespected by the majority of my older siblings, and because of it, I made it a point not to do as they did. I never like disrespecting my parents. I always thought to myself, "If I disrespect my parents as the others did, they would be devastated." They had already been through so much that it would have broken their hearts had I cross the line with them. They had been through enough pain and suffering. God help us all. I thank God for keeping me humble and never allowing me to disrespect my parents. I'm not sure I would have been able to live with this. Needless to say, I wasn't perfect with my parents, but I was careful to give them the respect they deserved. Regardless of what Dad may have done, whether right or wrong, I learned early on in life that parents are to be respected at all times. Anne never gave them anything to worry about; she was a saint compared to the rest of us.

Things at home were spiraling out of control for too long now, and no one ever offered help. No, not one person came to the rescue. Sometimes people don't like getting involved because they're not sure how the recipients will react. There were many other families in our communities going through the same things as we were. Though some families were a bit more careful, no one was exempt from the problems we all had living in the projects. No one wanted to talk about it. It was personal and delicate to talk about it among friends (parents). Just about every family living in both communities (Dayton Street and Seth Boyden projects) were affected one way or the other. Many family members or friends turned a blind eye and kept to themselves, not knowing what to do. Where were our friends when we really needed them? They were nowhere to be found. Everybody was on their own doing their own thing. My parents felt all alone in all of this. Everything around us turned to chaos. Things were worsening as the days went by, my parents continued drinking more and more, and my siblings continued their use of recreational drugs. Satan had us all bound; he had no mercy. We had no hope for anything. These were days of hell on planet earth for me and my family. Satan was lurking his claws at our doors (our hearts). Only Anne and I, the two youngest (two out of seven siblings), had been doing our best to please our parents. For the most part, we submitted and succumbed to our parents' wishes. We went to school, didn't cut class (skip school), and came home right after school, did our homework, got good grades, and stayed out of any real trouble. That is until I started messing up at Malcolm X. Shabazz High School in Newark before being transferred to Barringer High School. I'll talk a bit on this later on in another chapter.

If you lived in the projects, chances were that sooner or later, you, your siblings, and friends would probably experience drugs and get high on them. Everybody was experimenting with drugs and alcohol. At this point in time, Kato and Cheche were starting to live their lives in and out of jails, especially Cheche. Every time the family went out to visit my siblings behind bars, they promised that when the parole board would release them, they would not repeat the crime(s) again. But once they were out of jail, they break their promises and end up right back to where they started: locked up behind bars. That's because drugs was much stronger then their own will powers. They really wanted to keep their good behaviors, but Satan made sure they wouldn't keep their promises.

My brothers were well liked by many in the communities, especially with the lovely ladies. Kato had a really nice girlfriend, and they loved being around each other, but then parted ways and finalized their relationship. In many ways, he had become like my older brother Cheche.

Cheche and Kato were both dealing drugs, but I think they both consumed more than what they actually sold. Their drug habits were too expensive. It had become their way of life. They were big disappointments to my parents. My parents tried hard to get them to change but weren't successful in doing so.

-10-

TURNING FOURTEEN

It was the summer of 1972, two months after my fourteenth birthday, and at the end of the school year, I officially got my first summer job. I was underage, so my parents had to sign a consent form. It was one of those summer jobs that the City of Newark established for all teenagers who wanted to work for the summer. I believe it was only for teenagers from the ages of fourteen through eighteen. These were called the Summer Speedy Jobs, and my pay was about $120 on a biweekly basis." I got to work this job for three consecutive summers until I turned sixteen. The job was held in my own community and consisted of cleaning debris throughout the community playground and keeping clean the building in which I resided. All my friends living in the community had been doing the same exact thing. Every first weekend after payday, we get together and ride the bus to downtown Newark, and once there, we did our shopping. All the stores were located off of Broad and Market Street. The following weekends after our second pay, we would take the bus to Sea Side Heights and ride all the rides on the beach carnival. We did this almost every time we got pay. My friends and I knew lots of girls, but I was a bit shy back then, so I didn't really date much; I only dated two of the girls from our communities: one from Dayton projects and the other from Seth Boyden, and not until I was seventeen, I didn't do any real dating. I loved working, making money, and dressing up. I always gave Mom money and took the rest for shopping and kept some spending money in my pocket. Also, we loved going to see a movie at the one-dollar theatre located in the downtown area, and our favorite movies were all kung fu movies.

I was growing up fairly quickly, and so I wanted to look handsome for the ladies. In OKH, my friends and I went together to the liquor stores, bought beers, and hang out at the playground or inside the buildings while drinking beer and smoking marijuana (also known as pot, weed, grass, or joints and a nickel bag). If one of us didn't have any money, the rest of us chipped in to buy the booze and the pot we needed to get high. We always shared with one another. That's just how it was living in the projects. If there was a neighborhood party, we all made it our business to be there, even uninvited. I didn't know how to dance during my teenage years, but I still enjoyed watching others on the dance floor. Meanwhile, I did whatever I had to do to be accepted among my peers. Maybe it was peer pressure, but I didn't care. As long as I felt like I belong, I partake with whatever everybody else did. As long as there weren't any hard drugs, I hang with them everywhere. I only used marijuana and beer, and if any of my friends did hard drugs, well, I let them be and go about my business. I wanted nothing to do with hard drugs, and I didn't allow my friends to influence me with any of it. It was between fourteen and sixteen when I first started messing around and doing things of which I'm not proud of today.

I started off drinking Colt 45 beer and bumped it up to smoking weed. We got high a lot at Dayton Street School's playground. During the winter, we always smoked weed inside the project buildings to avoid the outside cold. During the summer months, we gathered around the projects' outside sitting areas, listening to our disco and Latin music while smoking joints and drinking beer while others snorted cocaine. We spent hours out there goofing off. Some of us liked to practice dancing with partners, others sang with their earphone gadgets on, and others conversed, laughed, and said jokes. It was like this every day during the summer months. Sometimes we hung at friends' apartments (those that were able to) and party for hours. This was how things roll in the projects, and if you wanted to fit in with the crowd, you then would join in on the parade.

I started smoking cigarettes behind my parents back at age sixteen. One day, while with a good friend of mine, we decided that I needed to stop by the house—my parents' apartment, where I lived—to pick up something. Dad had been suspicious about me smoking cigarettes, and as soon as we entered the premises, Dad checked me for cigarettes, and since he didn't find any, he decided to check my friend. Mind you, he had no right to check my friend's pockets, but he did. He started questioning him to see if they were mine, and my friend kept saying they were for his mom. Had Dad known that the pack of cigarettes belonged to me, he would have beaten me within an inch of my life. Thank God my friend had covered for me; otherwise, all hell would have broken loose. My dad was no dummy, and I knew all along that he had been suspicious of me, so I asked my friend to hold on to the cigarettes for me. After we left the premises, we laughed it off, but my friend was flabbergasted that my dad actually checked his pockets. He was like, "Wow, you were right, I can't believe he actually did that to me." I was like, "I told you so." My dad was something else. My friend and I never forgot about this. To this day, we still talk about it. Sometime later, after some months passed by, my dad allowed me to smoke in front of him; I was the age of sixteen.

I quit smoking cigarettes about some five years later. Every cigarette package has a clear warning on it that says, "Warning: dangerous to your health." It just isn't good for us, and it destroys our lungs and our health. Did you know that the Bible warns us not to take anything for our bodies that's going to harm it because if we do, God would destroy us (1 Corinthians 3:16-17 and 1 Corinthians 6:19-20)?

I had many good friends, and at times, I admit that some of the guys I hung around with were always up to no good. Hanging around the wrong kind of people caused me to stay out late many times, and this started to become a huge problem with my dad. I started hanging around the streets with my friends, and every time we had a chance, we buy a nickel bag of marijuana, rolled it into about seven to ten joints, and passed it around among us. Eventually, one thing led to another, and before we knew it, some of our friends whom are no longer with us (dead & buried), took things up a notch or two, which then led to other drugs such as heroin and/or snoring cocaine and shooting dope. They lost all control and become hard core junkies. That's exactly what the devil wants, so that he can take our souls to the pits of hell; though, I'm not saying that my friends went to hell just because they died before their time due to substance abuse. In no way am I saying that. I leave that to God. I've seen some of my family members and friends as well surrendering their hearts to God via Christ even in their darkness hour, therefore, I'll let God be the judge of who goes to heaven and who does not (Romans 14:10-11).

As a youth, I enjoyed playing basketball and other sports, though basketball was my favorite; I played it well. Dad was starting to worry about me. His concerns were that I would go astray just like my older siblings. At times, I would go straight home with my eyes looking like fireballs from the high of smoking marijuana. This was one of the side effects of smoking marijuana. Dad knew and suspected I had been doing something, but he just couldn't pinpoint what it was that I was doing. Other times, before going home, I would pour eye drops and cleared them up from the redness of the marijuana, but even so, my eyes turned like bee-bee eyes—really small. I never wanted to hurt my parents and/or God for that matter. I feared God and had always concerned myself with how both God and my parents thought about me. This was something I could never shake off and I'm grateful to God for that. There's a verse in the Bible that I believe I can apply to my life in regards to this kind of thinking. The author of the book of Hebrews writes in the New Testament, "Are not all angels ministering spirits sent to serve those who will inherit salvation?" (Hebrews 1:14, NIV).

God already knows who is going to respond to his calling and who isn't. God knew my heart, though I had been doing some things that were wrong I still believed in him and in his Son Jesus. Although I was lost in my sins, God knew that I would one day surrender my heart to him.

The Lord has his personal guardian angels looking out for us who know him, and for those that are being saved. Though I had not been walking in God's ways, it didn't mean that I didn't fear God or love him. I was only ignorant of him. The psalmists tell us that, "The angel of the Lord encamps around those who fear him, and he delivers them" (Psalms 34:7, NIV).

I must admit that God's mercy has always been upon me. It was nothing I did. It was what his Son Jesus had done for us all. He died for us and shed his blood on the cross for all of us.

Though I did the things I did, I had determined in my heart not to turn out like my other siblings. My siblings had been addicted to dope and were wasting their lives away. Nevertheless, Satan still had total control of the Vargas family, and I'm guilty as sin. Any righteousness I thought I had was as filthy as rags, and according to God, I was just as bad as the rest of my siblings—a sinner. Sin is sin, and God judges it all the same. Even so, I never really disrespected my parents. What I'm really saying is that though I may have been doing some things wrong, I always treated them with respect. On the other hand, my brothers were the total opposite. I really couldn't blame my dad for getting on my case. When parents care, that's what they do. So for that, I will always be grateful to Dad because, in a way, it really helped me along the way.

I enrolled late into high school, at the age of sixteen, and the first high school I attended was Malcolm X. Shabazz (formerly known as South Side High). It was there where I did my first year (ninth grade) but stayed back a year for cutting class (staying out of school). The school was in the southward part of Newark, and this was where I really got into trouble; I started off good but ended up bad. Things took a turn for the worst for me. I may have challenged my father, but it was nothing in comparison to what my siblings had put my parents through. This for sure added to their problems, and instead of attending my classes, I had been hanging out with my friends, and started going to many sets.

"Sets" were another word we liked to use instead of saying "party," but that's exactly what it was—a party. In these parties, we all shared marijuana, beer, and other drugs. Satan had been gradually sinking his claws into me as he did my other siblings. This had become the norm for me and for many of my friends. It's a venture without hope. Some of us were lucky enough to make it, but others weren't so lucky. I had gone from being an honorable student to becoming nothing and a dishonoring student to my parents and my teachers. I did the exact opposite of what I said I wouldn't do. I had become a victim of my own words. Satan had been gaining the upper hand on my life, and with the peer pressure, things sure weren't helping out at all.

Peer pressure is one of the worse things that can happen to any teenager. My life had been going backward instead of forward. Parents should always talk to their children just to make sure everything is okay with them, especially about school, sex, and drugs. Although my parents never adviced me on these issues, I still don't blame them for it. It was something that happened, and in our own way, each of us had to cope with it and learn to make the best of it. Back then, many parents had the same problems. The fact that I never had a real relationship with my father didn't help the matter. I think that if I would have been closer with Dad and if he would have sought to show any interest in me and what I had been doing, things may have turned out differently, although I thank God that things did turn out for the best for me. He was my dad only because I was from his seed, but that was as far as it went. He never talked to me to see how I had been doing or if I needed any help with my homework.. He never went to a school game to watch any of us succeed in any of the sports we were involved in and neither did Mom. Dad only spoke to me when he needed to scold me and reprimand me. Other than that, it's as if I didn't exist. Many parents wonder why their children don't hear them out. Well, gee, you got to get involve with them, partake in their activities, and be in their lives.

Dad started punishing me, and things were only heating up for me because I had been paying the price for the actions of my older siblings. He took out on me what he couldn't do to them, so I paid for their crimes. I guess it was expected being the youngest boy at home and the fact that Dad couldn't control my siblings any longer, it didn't help me a bit. Older siblings have no idea what they cause their parents to do to their younger siblings. Anne was in the same high school with me, but she was good. She may have cut class here and there, but for the most part, she was attending school and had good grades and passing. She didn't give my parents anything to worry about. On the contrary, my dad was harassing Anne, making her uncomfortable around him and made her life a living hell.

One of the ways my dad would punish me was by first putting some rice on the floor and making me get on my knees; it was excruciating pain. At the end of the hour, his buckle belt was the next thing I felt. At times he'd spanked me with his hand, and I know he meant well, just that he was a bit too much with his strictness. I've forgiven him and have no resentments in my heart toward him. Forgiveness is a very powerful tool and a very beautiful one. It releases love, removes hatred, and cast out any fears lingering in our hearts (Matthew 6:14-15).

Though my dad had been the way he was with me, I admit and confess that I appreciate everything he was trying to teach me. He had been through enough with my siblings, and he didn't want me going down the same road and path they did. Because of it, he did what he thought was best for me at the time. It wasn't the best way to deal with a son,but I guess it was the only way he knew how to deal with me.

Lulu's Sexual Abuse

Many years later and unbeknown to me, I learned about Lulu's sexual abused, i.e., raped, in the elevator of building six of Dayton projects. According to a dear and trusted family member, it happened as follows: She was hanging out to about three o'clock in the morning that night when this incident occurred. After being sexually abused, she immediately ran upstairs to a friend's apartment where my brother Cheche had been hanging out with some friends. She knocks on the door, and as soon as the door opened, she rushed in hysterically crying and tells my brother Cheche what had just happened to her. Cheche and Lulu were inseparable (Cheche always had her back). As soon as my brother heard the news, he exclaimed a few foul words and shot out the door, searching for the man who had just finished abusing my sister. I don't know how in the world my brother Cheche found the rapist, but when he did, he beat him so bad that he nearly killed the guy. Cheche then proceeded to kill him with his pistol, but for whatever reason, his gun would not go off. I doubted if my sister or my brother ever called the authorities on this man. My sister Lulu was private and didn't like talking about certain things, especially since my brother Cheche had taken care of it already. She didn't want to bring pain and hurt to the family, so she kept it quiet and kept it just between her, Cheche, and another sibling in confidence.

I like to say that God was in this scenario. God didn't want my brother spending the rest of his life in jail due to this man's evil deeds against my sister. I just hope and pray that if this guy is still alive, may he find peace and repentance before my God and asked him to forgive him for what he did to Lulu. In my heart, I have already forgiven him, but who knows how many other women he has victimized and scarred with his evil deeds, and i.e., if he's still living? God forgives all sins as long as we truly repent and mend our ways with God. God never turns away a repented heart. The prophet Ezekiel in the scriptures informs us about these things (Ezekiel 18:21–23).

> In the New Testament we are told that, "Jesus Christ is the same yesterday and today and forever" (Hebrews 13:8, NIV).
>
> This was the kind of environment we all lived in, subjected to all sorts of crimes, drugs, sex, and violence. But people like the man who raped my sister are sick individuals and need to be removed from society and placed behind bars with proper counseling. Otherwise, they will continue their evil quest and will stop at nothing. Satan uses these kinds of people to harm and destroy many innocent lives across the globe, but only Jesus can truly deliver them (John 10:10).

ALERT MODE

We should never look the other way if we suspect or know someone is trying to harm a love one, or even a friend. We are to be alert, stand our ground, and take immediate action before the enemy attacks. I can tell you the many countless times sick men followed me around in my younger years as a child and during my young adult years. These sick men followed me on foot, inside shopping malls, and many times around, while driving in their vehicles. They stopped me many times and boldly asked me to hop into their cars for a ride with them. Countless times I had to run for my life and encountered many frightened moments. They followed me to school and to work. But I knew better, and by the grace of God, I was always able to get away from them. These men wanted to rape me and hurt me and only God knows what else. I acknowledged that no harm ever came to me because God in heaven never allowed it, and I thank him for that. But there are many who aren't so lucky.

-11-

ANNE: THE PRINCESS AND HOUSEHOLD SAINT

There's Anne, the youngest of seven siblings and a loving sister. Anne was a saint. She didn't bother anybody or got in any kind of trouble. She was always delicate, sensitive, but loving. She mined her own business, had few friends, and respected our parents. The few friends she surrounded herself with were really good to her; they were amazing. Nowadays, it isn't so easy to find good friends like the ones Anne hung out with. There's a saying, "A friend is a dollar in your pocket," and that's so true, but that wasn't the case for little Anne. She had a good rapport among her friends and her peers. She confided in them, and together they kept their little secrets within their own little circle. They helped each other cope with some of the difficulties they each were having at their homes. Each one had their own personal problems, some more then others, but they all had them. Dad was strictly on edge with Anne, and for whatever reason, he gone a bit off the wall with her, causing her to discombobulate her nerves. Poor Anne was always a nervous wreck around Dad. All the harassing and nonsense had only become a nuisance to Anne, and resentment grasp hold of her poor little heart. Instead of making her feel special, he made her feel as if she was nothing.

Not even a daughter. He created animosity around her, and even so, she was still obedient. There were things that she as a child and as a daughter she would never succumb to. But Dad did not make her feel that she was loved. He made her feel as if she was the ugly duckling of the house. No father should ever cause his daughter to feel unwanted and unloved. More than that, no father should ever mistreat his daughter. Anne was such a good girl and was very close to Mom. She always tried to find comfort in Mom's arms, but Mom was oblivious to many things. Had it not been for her best friends, I'm not sure that Anne would have been sane today. Thank God for friends. Anne had been living a nightmare around Dad. It was a living hell for Anne, frustrating and excruciating. Dad just didn't know how to treat her with fatherly love.

By this time, Anne was agitated all the time with his constant threats and harassments. He had been coming home drunk after hanging out in bars with his drinking buddies then got ridiculously foolish at home. He picked a lot on Anne because she always defended Mom from Dad's interrogations. Dad always had the bad habit that when he drank too much, he felt that he needed to know everything that was going on at home. He accused Anne of covering up for Mom to the point that if Anne said that wrong thing, he hit on her here and there and mentally and emotionally abused her. He said many wrong things to her, and he always accused both Anne and Mom of anything and everything. It was as if his mind was strictly fixed on harassing Anne all the time, accusing her of being just like Mom (whatever that meant). It's like the drinking had seriously complicated his mine implicating his frame of thought with perplexity. Dad no longer could keep it together. The majority of his arguments with Mom and Anne were fabrications from all his drunkenness. Fabrications Satan created in his mind from all the alcohol he had been consuming. Mom sort of had to keep her distance from Dad because he was constantly agitating her with his ridiculous questions; they were just absurd. As always, Dad would then turned to Anne to question her about whatever Mom said to him, and if Anne's responses to his questions weren't what he wanted to hear (they were more like interrogations), he immediately get defensive with Anne then scold her and send her to her room after saying a few inappropriate things to her. He acted as if both Mom and Anne were lying to him or hiding things from him. Whatever Mom or Anne had to say, he disregarded because he never believed them. To makes things worse, he named called Anne inappropriate names that were hurtful and appalling. He treated her as if she were insufficient and a nobody. This was a direct violation from a father to his daughter.

Unfortunately, the name-calling didn't stop, and neither did the drinking. His threats were continuously harboring hatred into Anne's delicate heart, causing chaos between him and Mom. He scoffed at both Mom and Anne as if they were always doing wrong making them feel insignificant. I mean, he's even talking to Mom as if she was his daughter and not his wife. Mind you, Mom was the mother of his seven children. The booze really had him going really bad. He wanted to separate the relationship that both Mom and Anne had with each other; they were emotionally attached to each other and Dad disliked that about them. His false accusations and mistreats worsened every day. The drinking blocked his mind, not allowing Dad to think straight. Satan had gotten control over Dad from all the alcohol he had been consuming, and the problems continued to soar in.

Dad was simply paranoid and got out of control. The only time he was calm was whenever he was sober. Other than that, he would freak out and say the unimaginable.

For those that don't understand, drinking habits distort our ways. We need to be extremely careful with how we consume alcohol. The apostle Paul writes in the New Testament, "Stop drinking only water, and use a little wine because of your stomach and your frequent illnesses" (1 Timothy 5:23, NIV). But darn, he said "just have a little wine," and he meant it. Wine wasn't made for us to engage in it so that we can go merry and lose control. It was made so that we can be happy with life, i.e., a merry heart (Ecclesiastes 10:19). There's a big difference. Solomon writes in the Old Testament, "Wine is a mocker and beer a brawler; whoever is led astray by them is not wise" (Proverbs 20:1). In fact, Paul warned us in the New Testament, "Do not get drunk on wine, which leads to debauchery. Instead, be filled with the Spirit" (Ephesians 5:18, NIV).

Many times at home, disagreements between Dad and Mom caused Dad to rage out on my dear sister. Anne's spirit had been suppressed by Dad's constant threats and his drinking problem. She being the youngest and a girl, what could she do? Mom was sort of powerless and everyone else was in their own little world, including me and that was probably because I was always outdoors. When a father mistreats a child, what he gets in return is anything but love (Colossians 3:21).

Only at times, Dad would be nice to Anne, but there was too much hurt in Anne's heart for her to even try to warm up to him. By this time, he had already created too much emotional damage, and Anne's poor little heart was broken. He really made things difficult for her. That's the worst thing a father can do to his little princess. Unfortunately, Daddy's little girl never felt like a princess. Dad was way too stern with all of us and whatever he said was "law." Drinking habits have always been the cause of stupid things, but not everything can be blamed on the drinking. We have to take responsibility for our actions. Anne suffered and cried in silence in her room from Dad's awful mistreatments. She locked the door behind her and cried her heart out. It was as if our father had taken his anger out on her. There were too many times that she felt very uncomfortable around Dad. Dad never knew how to express his affection toward any one of us. We knew he loved us, but he just never knew how to demonstrate it. The pains and hurts and the sufferings that followed our lives turned into hateful resentments, and I can go on and on. Children need the love of their parents, and when a parent mistreats his or her child, all hope is flushed down the John, metaphorically speaking, leaving no expectations for anything good to look forward to. That's the kind of damage that this can create between parents and children. Discipline your child only when time calls for it. If you love your child and/or children, demonstrate your parental love to them. The damage caused by this phenomenon across this nation is a sin in itself. This is sin that God will judge and bring justice to. Children are from God and an inheritance to parents from the Lord (Psalms 127:3). For those of you that have adopted or foster any children, the same applies to you.

Anne was always a special child with special needs, and special children need special attention. Anne had been born with some health difficulties and had always been fragile. I won't go into all the details, but Dad's stereotyping her didn't help a bit. I like to say that with God, she is still special and God will always love her. God will always give Anne that special love that she never had growing up at home. He will never abandon her or mistreat her as if she was less than others. Friends, when love is lacking in a child's life, and it isn't permeating from his or her parent, the child's brain cells become fused, confused, and it leaves no room for trust, making the child feel unsafe and insecure. The love of a parent makes a significant impact on their child's mine and character. Otherwise, an attitude of rebellion will form and gradually deteriorate within the child's heart, and their minds are corrupted beyond repair, unless we seek out help for the child. It can affect their walk at life in ways unimaginable, therefore, love your child and demonstrate it with actions.

Have you ever asked yourself, why is it then that people drink? Many drink because they think it will help them forget their problems, but in all reality, it doesn't. The more booze they drink, the more they remember their problems. Alcohol can be an extremely dangerous source of a lifestyle, and if a person can't get a grip on his or her life, it will destroy them, and everything they ever work so hard for will vanish. There are too many wounds rooted deep within our souls that if I were to bring some to surface, Satan himself may try twisting them around to suit his evil schemes. They are just too painful to bring to memory. My objective is to bring you to a Christ-like mind, so that your thinking gives way to clarity. Having a renewed mind with the word of God brings acceptance, love, and forgiveness. A mind that's renewed by the word of God learns to forgive those by whom they have been hurt. They even learn to forgive themselves for anything they may have done, and/or, for feeling that they were at fought for all the things that happened to them by those who hurt them and mistreated them. The enemy likes to make them feel and think that they were the ones at fought, but that isn't so in many cases, and especially in Anne's case.

-12-

MY BROTHER CHECHE

Cheche decides to shack up with (to live together unmarried) a girlfriend at home in our parents' apartment. She was of a different race and Dad had a really hard time accepting her as my brother's girlfriend. To add insult to injury, the poor girl was also addicted to drugs. Both she and Cheche had been getting high together on hard drugs. They had been shooting dope and using lots of heroin and cocaine. Although, they stayed outdoors all day long and out of Dad's way, it was still very bothersome to Dad because he knew they were both wasting their lives away at doing nothing productive aside of using drugs. Dad felt they were only going to havoc more problems at home. Meanwhile, Dad's frustrations were mounting up and every time both Cheche and his girlfriend entered the apartment, Dad's facial expression changed just by the condition both Cheche and his girlfriend were in; they were always drugged up. Mom suffered as well. Both Mom and Dad had to ponder many things in their hearts in order not to stir things up. It wasn't too hard reading their minds and thoughts. Anger suppressed their spirits, and tensions between Dad and my brother intensified. Dad didn't really know what else to do, so he asked Cheche to leave with his girlfriend and not to come back home. He demanded that they go and find their own place and go do whatever the heck they wanted to do.

Dad just couldn't take it anymore. It was too much for him to handle. Cheche was really becoming too dangerous, so asking him to leave with his girlfriend was no longer an option. It was the only solution Dad thought of at the time, and for that, I sure don't blame him. No parent should ever have to put up with this kind of stuff from their own children. After all, Dad had his own demons to deal with and having to deal with my brother's only complicated matters.

Mind you, it was my parent's apartment, but Cheche didn't care a bit about that. He was in complete defiance, and Dad was hopeless in dealing with him. Cheche didn't care what my parents had to say. He listened to Mom a bit, but when it came to Dad, he wouldn't have it. It's as if Mom always knew how to say things to him. No doubt, Cheche loved Mom and despised our dad. Cheche always did whatever he felt like, and no one could tell him what to do. Nevertheless, he moved out with his girlfriend for a while. According to the scriptures, living together without being legally married is considered sin. God calls it adultery and fornication. Such sins God will judge among men and many more. He disapproves of them and condemns these kinds of behavior (Deuteronomy 5:18, Numbers 25:6–13, and Galatians 5:19–21).

I like to say that even though my brother's girlfriend may have been an addict, she was also a very nice girl. She didn't bother anybody. Whenever she came in from outdoors, she was always courteous, quite, and to herself. Dad just didn't like her because of the drug problem she had and because she was of a different race.

Dad was sort of an old-fashioned guy. He believed that we have to stick to our own kind. As far as he was concerned, mixing with other races was considered taboo. But he didn't understand that to us (his children), it didn't really matter as long as it was the opposite sex. Every time they came home, it was usually during the late night hours in order to evade Dad's confrontations. For the most part, Dad was always awake and alert when my brother came in from outdoors with his girlfriend. Drugs had been destroying Cheche's way of thinking and no matter what Dad or anyone else tried telling him, he disregarded it all. In fact, he got agitated whenever Dad or anyone tried talking to him. He didn't like it and didn't want to hear it. A few times, the authorities stopped by with warrants for his arrest, but it seemed that every time they came by, he outwitted them as if he knew their every move. They had such a hard time catching up to him. He moved from place to place, evading the cops until he knew that things were safe for him to return home, even though Dad had asked him to leave. But he kept coming back to us, after Dad had already kicked him out with his girlfriend; this time his girlfriend stayed away. He was one swift guy; though at the end, he eventually paid with his life. Unfortunately, he had been doing so many wrong things throughout his young adult years, and this due to his drug addiction. By this time, Cheche had completely changed and was no longer the same person we all knew to be our sibling and son to our parents. His mind was distorted from the use of so many drugs.

Every opportunity brother Cheche got, he get out there and steal and rob from people of all sorts of life. Regardless who they were, he just didn't care. He didn't value their lives and put at risk their lives including his own. Many times he held people at gunpoint. He stripped them penniless, taking from them all their valuable possessions and threatening their lives, if they were to say anything to the authorities or anyone. This was his way of life. He was completely out of control, and everywhere he went, he fined himself a way to commit some sort of atrocity. He couldn't be trusted. Mom kept praying for him the only way she knew how. Though I wasn't much of a religious person, I try and follow her example.

Brother Cheche was always happy whenever he got his hands on some money. He knew that as long as he had money in his pocket, he can get himself a fixed—drugs (to shoot dope), and that's all he cared about. It was evident that he had become his own enemy and dangerous to himself and to others causing threat and harms throughout many communities, and at times even to those he surrounded himself with. Drugs had really taken him to a different level. It drove him to do things that he himself would have never imagined. When he wasn't high, he was asleep, and when he wasn't asleep, he was high. How sad to have to live a life like this. The only time he was actually really sober from drugs and crimes was when he was behind bars. Other than that, he lived a horrible life of drugs and crime. There were times he actually stayed home watching some TV programs or movies. Those days he usually stayed calm. He was a nice young man with a great personality. But the darned drugs had him in a different world altogether. This is not what God had intended for Cheche. God wanted to bless him, but Cheche kept on pressing forward with his own life of drug addiction

Over the course of time, Cheche was bringing home thousands of dollars from many breaking and entries (breaking and robbing into houses and businesses). He had been committing robberies and breaking into many private homes and forcefully taking cash, jewelry, and other valuables from his terrified victims. Afterward, he would come home, all drugged up and flaunt money around us, as if he were celebrating in victory his crimes against his victims. Whenever the authorities stopped by the house, they informed my parents that they needed to find a way to bring Cheche in. In other words, they wanted my parents to talk to my brother and have him surrender to the authorities. He had terrorized too many communities and the police had had enough of my brother. He had been committing horrendous crimes. The authorities had been looking for him for sometime now but were futile in catching him. Unless one of us would give him up, the authorities were helpless in apprehending him. Everyone was starting to worry. The police had already informed us various times that if something wasn't done soon, and if he couldn't be apprehended by law enforcement, either Cheche was going to end up killing somebody, someone would probably kill him, and/or that law enforcement would probably end up hurting him on a chase or even killing him in a shootout if he try resisting arrest.

In fact, he even got my sister Lulu to join in as an associate, and various times, they both went out together and held innocent victims at gunpoint. It was nothing but a nightmare for those victimized.

Cheche and his friends started carrying guns with them more than the usual. They had gotten to the next level of crimes and felt the need to carry weapons for any extra protection. Giving the crimes they were committing, they weren't taking any chances. They were notorious for braking in houses and having mercy on no one. Drugs had consumed their minds and ate away at them like gangrene. Clearly, their minds were far gone; they didn't think any more. They acted on whatever atrocities came to mind. As far as their friends were concerned, Cheche and his buddies were nothing but trouble.

Despite all the mishaps my family and I were having at home, we had many friends that got along well with us and loved being around us. Many of our families and friends lost loved ones to drugs, guns, and crime. Some of our friends were gunned down just because. Others looked for trouble. Others got killed for dealing with the wrong people and some for a bad deal. Some were killed for not paying up and for some for a dope deal gone wrong, and all of it for pure stupidity. Unfortunately, others were in the wrong place at the wrong time.

All things can be expected when living in the projects. Dayton Street projects had many good families living in the them.

While we were still in the projects, during the summer months, we all went and hung out at the Dayton Street School playground. It had a nice swimming pool for the two communities—OKH and Seth Boyden projects. The school also had a set of large giant steps leading from one playground to the other where we all played baseball, stickball, and got high together. For many of us, it's where the booze, marijuana, and drugs had been introduced to us. It's were many of the guys learned to play handball, good baseball, and basketball. Our favorite was when we played, stickball. We all loved playing stickball, especially when we were high.

Many parents were stressed with everything that had been happening around them. Things were just crazy in the projects. After some years, just about all the projects in Newark had gotten corrupted. Some turned into pure jungles. This was a tragic because the projects in Newark were once one of the nicest places to live in. Many good families started moving away to private homes, and those that stayed behind were challenged with all kinds of troubles.

-13-

MARY'S MARRIAGE

While all this had been going on, my oldest sister Mary remarried and gave birth to two lovely daughters. The first infant was born with disabilities and was admitted to an institution for special needs children out of Massachusetts, but after a few years died. She went home to be with the Lord. My brother-in-law was well-liked by everyone and all those that surrounded themselves around him loved him. He was an easygoing guy. Mary met him at a party via his brothers. I was around fourteen years old when she married him. She married him on my mother's birthday, August 22. Their wedding ceremony was beautiful, and both were excited to start their new lives together. They rented a nice size wedding hall and celebrated their vows with wine and music and had a live Latin salsa band playing for them. Mary looked happy and absolutely gorgeous on her wedding day. The groom was the happiest man walking the planet that day. He was so in love with my sister and did anything for her. My parents were especially happy for them and extremely fond of him. They knew Mary had been through a lot and were wishing that this time around, things would get better for her. They felt that with a good man at her side, she was finally going to live the life she always desired to live and get whatever she wanted. My parents loved her husband and thought very highly of him. He was hardworking and of a gentle spirit. He loved traveling and going places and having fun. He provided for my sister and her child (Tony), and treated him with love and respect as if he was his own flesh and blood.

His trade was in automechanics, and he did well for a living—financially. His employers loved him and loved that he worked hard and got his job done. He came from a good family and was well-mannered. He treated all of us with respect and loved my family. He was a good man, and it didn't take me long to love him as a brother. He didn't care about my sister's past and delighted in taking great care of her and Tony. Tony also loved him and enjoyed having his new dad around. They went a lot to the movies and at times took me along. After the movie theater, we all loved going out to eat at a diner in Harrison, New Jersey. Harrison Diner was located along side East Newark, New Jersey—right across the bridge and parallel to McCarter Highway. For a time, everything had been going well for them as a marriage should. They seemed happy and enjoyed each other's company doing things together as married couples should be doing. Their relationship had been growing strong, and they had been moving forward with their lives as all marriages should. Gradually, their relationship changed, and their marriage started falling apart. They were living in building six of Dayton projects, from there moved to a house a few blocks away from the buildings right on Dayton Street, and when things really heated up in their marriage, they decided to relocate and moved out to the Vailsburg area of Newark, located on the west end of Newark, near his place of employment.

-14-

MOVING OUT OF DAYTON STREET PROJECTS

My parents moved us out of Dayton Street projects in the year 1974 and moved us back to Seventh Avenue projects where we had lived many years before. By this time, CCH had gotten much worse than when we first moved out when I was seven. I was glad to leave OKH, but not happy we had returned to our former residential community. We went from bad to worse. As I mentioned in chapter nine, I was sixteen at the time, and I had transferred from Malcolm X. Shabazz to Barringer High School. Mom joined Dad with the alcohol drinking before we moved out from Dayton, and things gotten worse. Turning to drinking was one of the worse decisions Mom had ever made. Now there was no one to keep Dad sane; they both needed help. Drinking didn't allow them to make the best of decisions. Mom's drinking started with friends that both she and Dad had been associating with. After a while, Mom was losing control and between her and Dad, things went from worse to chaos. They drank almost every day with their friends and half of the time they were coming home drunk. They loved drinking their wine, scotch, and rum.

Leaving OKH seemed like a good move for them because they only had to worry about me and my youngest sister Anne. Dad had pretty much excommunicated the rest of my siblings from our home, and so, everyone was on their own. They were tired of everything and thought that moving us away would help alleviate some of their problems. My parents were not alone on this. There were other families in the projects going through the same things, but many kept it to themselves. Some families never talked about their problems to anyone. Others turned the cheek as if everything was fine and nothing was wrong. Some were ashamed of their children while others just didn't care and others didn't know what to do. Just like my parents, the majority of the people living in the projects (not all) never sought professional help.

At times, we are all in need of some kind of help. Matthew writes in the New Testament, "Ask and it will be given to you; seek and you will find; knock and the door will be opened to you. For everyone who asks receives; he who seeks finds; and to him who knocks, the door will be opened" (Matthew 7:7–8, NIV).

Parents need to take initiative and set priorities and goals for themselves, but mostly for their children, and not burdened their children with their own responsibilities. They should always encourage their children to do better for themselves and give them the helping hand they need to get ahead in life and prosper (2 Corinthians 12:14-15).

-15-

SEVENTH AVENUE PROJECTS

Now that we were back to living in Seventh Avenue, we were about to face other challenges. This time around we were renting an apartment on the side of the Sheffield Drive section of the community and our apartment was on the twelfth floor. I was seven when we moved out of this community, and it's where I first learned to play the guitar. I wasn't too sure why my parents chose to return to these projects, but maybe it was because Mom had other relatives living here.. These were more dangerous than Dayton Street projects, and things were about to take a turn for the worse. I remembered hearing rumors about women being raped on the top floors, hallways, and stairways. Murders were taking place as well. One time when I was out on the playground with my friends, policemen were walking out from one of the buildings with body bags of dead people chopped in pieces. It was a haunting sight. I couldn't believe what I was looking at. Anne and I were still in high school and quickly made friends throughout the community and at the school. As always, Anne limited herself to a specific circle of friends in the community (mostly family), whereas, I made friends with everyone I could.

Anne didn't like living here too much, and for that, I couldn't blame her. It was dangerous living in these buildings and the fact that we didn't know a whole lot of people made it especially dangerous. We were always on an alert mode all the time. I already knew a few friends but even so, I didn't feel safe—at least not at the beginning. I had spent many weekends during the summer months at this community with a relative who lived here at the time. But Anne knew no one. I protected her, and we both walked together to school every day, and I made sure no one messed with her. After a while, we got used to living here, and things felt like we were living back at OKH. But for Anne, she never felt safe or secure living here. My parents moved us out of Dayton Street projects because they were having too many problems with my older siblings over there, yet they were oblivious to the fact that living in these projects only put our lives in more danger, especially for Anne. The same kinds of activities had been taking place here as they did back in Dayton Street projects. Drugs and all sorts of crimes had taken over the community. It just wasn't safe as when we first lived here when we were young children. Every now and then, someone was getting shot or killed; mostly, due to drug deals. Fights would break out every now and then, and people got hurt. Some people were just at the wrong place at the wrong time. Young ladies and women had to be careful not to be alone, especially in elevators. Living in these ghettos was not to be taken lightly.

The same problem we had in Dayton Street projects with the elevators, we had here. If the elevators in our building were out of service and we didn't feel like walking up the stairs to our floor, we would take the elevator at the adjacent attached building to ours and take the elevator up to the twelfth floor then walk up another flight of stairs up to the roof and walk across the top of the roof into our building. Once in our building, we would walk back down the stairs to our floor. It was better to do this than to have to walk up the stairs, especially if we were carrying grocery bags.

I hung around with cousins and with great friends and played lots of basketball. I had the most fun at Barringer High School, but it was here where I started using more marijuana and staying out of school a lot. Barringer High School had lots of Hispanics at the time and much of the students living in the area were all from north Newark where I ended up living with my parents a few years after leaving Seventh Avenue. Barringer High School was the center of my life during the first year of moving back to these projects. It's were I met most of my friends and gradually started going out to nightclubs and private house parties. Just about everyone I met was doing some sort of drugs. Every party I went to, my friends and I got stoned high on marijuana and on the booze, though we weren't too keen on the booze, but we drank it to avoid our mouths from getting dry from smoking so much marijuana. I met many young women at school. Between the ladies and the marijuana my life took a 380-degree turnaround, and I ended up dropping out of high school, never completing my second year. Mind you, I used to be an honorable student.

I lost interest in education and focused all my attention on ladies, dating, partying, and getting high. It seemed that for a while, I was following in the same footsteps of my older siblings.

Although I dropped out of high school, I went straight to work. Before dropping out of high school, I must have flirted with every girl there was. Many women were attracted to me, and the opportunities were endless. I had become sort of a gigolo during my tenure at Barringer High, and a great dancer, which in turn opened lots of sexy doors for me, metaphorically speaking. Dancing helped me approach women with easiness and a whole new world of sexual appetites opened up for me. I was a sociable kind of guy, outgoing, confident and made many friends. As my dancing skills improved, so did my sensual skills. The more I learned to dance, the more time I spent at nightclubs and private parties. I had become the center of attention at many nightclubs for my dancing skills. I loved dressing up sharply and dated as many ladies as possible throughout New Jersey.

My friends and I love hanging out at Branch Brook Park during high school hours with the ladies. Branch Brook Park was located directly behind the school, and it's were my friends and I spent most of our time goofing off. I especially loved coming to this park because of the childhood memories I had with my brother Kato; we had spent lots of time together in this park. Down the hill from the school was Willie's Candy Store. The store was known as Willie's Pool Room. Willie had own this store for a very long time, and by this time, he was in his sixties. I remembered being a kid when I was living in Sixth Avenue and he was already there. He was well known. The candy store had a pool table, and we loved playing eight ball and the arcade machines. This is one of the many things my friends and I did while skipping high school. The projects at Seventh Avenue had another corner store with a pool table and arcade machines where we spent much of our time. We were all over the place except for in school where we should have been. I got involved with too many women and everything started changing for me.

To make things worse, I ran into an old friend of mine from Dayton Street who had been doing lots of drugs. I started hanging with him every day and started using marijuana more frequently. The woman that surrounded us didn't make things any easier. Having lots of women didn't help my situation; it just added to it.

This added pressure and tension at home with my parents. I had disappointed my parents just like my other siblings. I once said that I wouldn't disappoint my parents by dropping out of school, yet I did the exact opposite of what I said I would never do. It is the choices we make and these were poor choices on my behalf, especially after being a good son to my parents and an honorable student. Our Creator wants us to do well, respect our parents, and study. But many times we get caught up in the wrong things and think we're better than thou, and before we know it, we become the very thing we once said and swore we wouldn't do. I was definitely the brother of my siblings.

Because of God's love and mercy toward me, He never allowed me to become a junkie. All my siblings had become junkies except for my second oldest sister, Luz, and my youngest, Anne. Other than that, all the rest of them had become junkies.

-16-

TURNING EIGHTEEN

I turned eighteen years old and celebrated it with my friends drinking Budweiser beers.

Though CCH wasn't the safest place to live in, I still made the best of things and got along well with friends in the community. For entertainment, my friends and I played full-court basketball while listening to music and getting high on grass. As soon as I turned eighteen, I registered to vote for the very first time as an American citizen; it made me feel important. As an American citizen, I believed in exercising my freedom of speech and all my God given rights as a citizen. I learned early on in life that the only way any individual had the right to fight for any cause was to be a registered voter if he or she wanted their voice heard. Despite all the little mishaps I had been wrongfully doing, I still had a sense of direction in my life and walked around with a good head on my shoulders. I knew I had done some stupid things, but it didn't mean that I wasn't any good to society.

One of the things that captivated me living in the projects was the sound of the Latin Salsa Beat. The Latin salsa sound was unbelievably amazing. This kind of music always fascinated me, and from the very first time my ears heard the beat, I immediately fell in love with it. It was here were I also learned to play the congas (percussion) and where the sound of the salsa beat really started to captured my heart. It was here where music became passionate to me, but even so, I still didn't play until years later after my conversion to Christianity, seven years later, and a year after my conversion.

While I was still eighteen, Dad hit me once for some stupidity, so I left home for about a week and crashed over my brother Kato's place. Kato by this time had his own pad (apartment), not too far from us, about a ten to fifthteen minute walk from the projects.

Imagine being eighteen and still getting hit at home by your parents? This is unheard of and yet I myself went through this with my dad. At that age, no parent should be doing such things. Do you know all the pain, resentment, and hurts an individual carries in their heart? The physical scars aren't the real problem. It is the emotional scars that are left behind in our hearts, which stick around for a long time, causing internal damage and emotional pain and confusion. That is not the way to discipline a young adult son or daughter. I know people today that are married and are still carrying these emotional scars. They just don't know how to let go.

Parents really need to learn how to treat and take care of their children the proper way. They should not abuse their children in this manner just because they're the parent. When parents do what's right for their children, nothing but blessings will follow behind. The author of the book of Proverbs writes in the Old Testament, "The righteous man leads a blameless life; blessed are his children after him" (Proverbs 20:7, NIV).

During this time, Mary and her husband occasionally came out to Seventh Avenue to visit us, but they were having major problems in their marriage. By this time, they had moved out of the Vailsburg area of Newark and rented an apartment in another private home in Clifton, New Jersey, with their two children, Tony and their baby girl. Their marriage had been in trouble for some time now, and their marriage continued to struggled. They really had a hard time trying to work things out.

As you read about Mary's life, follow her journey. Her life was one of many spirals—ups and downs. Mary definitely lived a rough life, one of many hardships and painful turmoil. But there was a powerful driving force riding Mary. Her life was a roller-coaster without any breaks, causing havoc and a life of mishaps where one looses complete control. The world of drugs and its temptations turned her marriage into a merry-go-round until it deteriorated.

Their marital struggles got worse every day until they separated and got a divorce. After their divorce, the husband took their baby girl to live with him in Puerto Rico, and he and his parents helped raised the child. After some time living in Puerto Rico, he remarried. His new wife then raised the child—my sister Mary's baby girl and Mary took her son Tony to live with her, and she raised him on her own.

Unfortunately, my sister Mary had been using drugs and it sucked the life right out of her. Her husband had tried everything he could in his power to save the marriage before divorcing her, but no matter what he did, my sister resisted. Unfortunately, it was the drugs that had her doing things she didn't really want to do. She couldn't help herself anymore and drugs got the best of her. Her life changed from being a housewife and mother to becoming a drug addict. Instead of taking care of her home and family, she was out in the streets doing drugs, throwing her life away. Nothing was the same any longer for Mary. She didn't want to give up her daughter, but she knew it was the only way her daughter would have a chance at life. She did a good decision in letting the father stay with the daughter. Besides, she needed help, though she didn't seek it at that time. She was too far gone with drugs. She kept digging herself deeper into that hard life of drugs, and it took her a long time to recuperate from them. Mary and her daughter keep in contact with each other and are both doing well. Her daughter is happily married with a daughter of her own and she completed her college education. Had she stayed behind in Newark with her mom, who knows what would have happened to her. God knows all things, and he knows what's best for all of us.

My family and I still stayed living in the projects. During this time, I was still having problems with Dad, and I couldn't go home. I had recently turned 20 and I found myself sleeping outside in the cold nights on the playground benches. Some nights were worse than others. I didn't have any money at the time and wasn't working until afterward. I've always been the type of guy that I didn't like asking anyone for anything, so sleeping late at night on the benches of Seventh Avenue became my new home for a while. One doesn't get much sleep outside on benches. It's a very scary thing to have to experience, and danger lurks all around you. These were dangerous times for me, yet, I managed to survive, and I knew things were somehow going to get better for me. There is no glory sleeping on a street bench and worries piled up in one's brain. Every day I had to think, when will I be able to get out of this situation? It only added more concerns. These were some of the things I went through living in the projects, as I always faced danger. The night chills and the loneliness that sets in are the worse. Somehow, I was always able to get my hands on a little money for a meal, and since there was a new Chinese Restaurant in the area, I always went there and got me a pint of shrimp fried rice throughout my duration living and sleeping at the benches. Gosh, it felt so good to be able to eat. After a few weeks, I found work and back to live with my parents. When I was sleeping at the benches, I remember there was a Pentecostal lady that allowed me to sleep over her house a few nights after learning that I was sleeping outside on benches. I thank my God for that and for her. In the New Testament, John writes that Jesus said that the world will know his disciples by the love of Christ that's in them. May the Lord bless her and all her family members for all the love and kindness she has shown me when I most needed it. After my parents decided to leave the projects, I followed behind them and lived with them at the new house, which Dad purchased on Delavan Avenue.

My family and I lived in Seventh Avenue projects for about three years after leaving the Dayton projects. We had relatives that stayed behind: they were some of my mother's siblings and their families and my deceased sister's (Luz) children living with their father and grandmother. Finally, after we moved to Delavan Avenue, my widower brother-in-law moved his entire family out of the projects, and later on my mother's siblings and their families left as well. My brother-in-law purchased a home on Summer Avenue in Newark. Summer Avenue was part of north Newark, and it wasn't too far from the projects. But it was a lot better than living in the projects. It was crazy that we were all living in the projects, but I admit that I learned a lot living in these projects. Our new home was further north from them about five minutes south from Belleville, New Jersey.

After my parents and I settled in our new home on Delavan Avenue, the rest of my siblings gradually followed and came back to live with us, after separating from their significant others, and barged in on our parents. My sister Anne and her husband moved in with us from their Broadway apartment in Newark, after they had been having some financial problems. Anne and her husband were seeing each other while we were living in Seventh Avenue, but had gotten married right before my parents moved us out to Delavan Avenue.

SPECIAL COMMENT

Not all people living in the projects are bad people. In fact, I have found that many of the people living in poor communities are of humble spirits and are good people trying to do their best to survive. These people need our prayers. Many people have made it successfully out of the projects and have moved on with their lives to bigger and better things, and their lives have changed for the better. I am a living testimonial. Therefore, contrary to popular beliefs, not all people living in the projects are evil people. Most importantly, God loves them as much as he loves us. God has been gracious to many of us, and therefore, we should be gracious to them. Many live there because they have no other means or resources to better themselves for a better life.

-17-

DELAVAN AVENUE

I was twenty when my parents moved us out of the projects and purchased their own one-family home on Delavan Avenue. Our house cornered with Summer Avenue, and down the other end was Broadway Avenue, which was the main strip, and we lived about a quarter of a mile from the border of Bellville, New Jersey.

We all had enough of the projects and were finally glad to move on with our lives away from the ghettos. After moving out, I had determined not to ever again return to live in the projects. This was the second home we ever owned since our last house in Paterson, and it felt so good to finally live in our own private house again. No more of the many unpleasant experiences. It was finally over; well not completely, but at least things were a whole lot better than living in the projects.

I had forgotten what it felt like to once again live in our own private house, but it sure felt great. On Broadway Avenue were all the main stores for shopping. Mary was in and out of the house days at a time due to her drug problem. Anne and her husband were still with us trying to resolve their financial and marital problems. Kato returned to live with us after spending some time in Puerto Rico, and Cheche returned as well. Lulu was in and out as well, but mostly spent her days out staying with other friends. We made friends with our neighbors, and Kato and

I quickly became popular with the ladies in the neighborhood. Cheche never hung around the neighborhood cause he was too busy with his drug life and only came home to sleep, shower, and eat. The neighborhood was nice, and everyone seemed to like us and befriended us quickly. Kato liked going in and out of the house, but at times, he liked sticking around just to flirt with the ladies in the neighborhood. Both Kato and I were the biggest flirts in the neighborhood, and we wasted no time in getting to know the ladies. My parents were well liked and quickly became friends with just about everyone on our block.

Kato and I were the new rivals on the block, and many of the guys were jealous when they saw we were getting lots of attention from the ladies. We both thought that we were God's gift to women. The ladies loved everything about us, so we pressed forward with the flirting. There was one exception, although Kato had his great looks; some of the ladies kept their distance from him due to his drug problem, but others really didn't care. They like messing around and getting high with him. Other than that, he was swift with the ladies and practically had any lady he wanted. Both Kato and I were the same when it came to women. Talking about having big heads, metaphorically speaking, we had all the women in the world we ever wanted. Being the new guys on the block gave us an advantage and headway over others.

We were always being invited to private house parties. As usual, we smoked pot, drank beer, and danced the night away. Kato wasn't much of a dancer, but he did danced a little, but with his looks, he didn't need to dance. Women followed him as they did me. We felt like we were in wonderland. We went to many of Newark's local bars and wherever we went, ladies were always interested in us and the opportunities were endless. Who would have thought me being a playboy or gigalo? We all knew Kato was flirtatious, but me, I was only getting started.

Meanwhile, my parents' lives did not improve a bit and their marriage was only worsening. Though we had moved far away from the projects, too much damage had already been done, and my parents had too many struggles. Things didn't help a bit that my other siblings gradually followed and moved back in with us. With all the things that were going on, chaos was starting to break out once again, and we became infamous and notorious in our neighborhood. That's the last thing my parents needed. They were drained both emotionally and physically. Feeling helpless as they did and still having problems only continued to deteriorate their marriage. It was as if there was no hope for them, and no way out. They couldn't find solutions to their problems. They were desperate and were constantly arguing about anything and everything; all due to many of my siblings' actions, i.e., inappropriate behaviors. Anne and her husband's problems continued to mount, and getting along for them had become extremely difficult. As I previously mentioned, my siblings gradually returned to live with us, and after about a year all my siblings had all been back home living as one big happy family. Well to the outsider that's what it may have seemed to be like, but we were far from *one big happy family*. Although things were different and we were adults, and a household of problems, it still felt great to be with one another as in the early days when we were all young, living at home with our parents. But the problems kept mounting, and my parents were losing their grip on their marriage as things were falling apart. Everybody was doing their own thing, and I was the only one at home who had a job helping my parents out. Dad was no longer working so any help I contributed to really came in handy, and mother worked as well.

Mary, Lulu, and Kato were all messing up big time with drugs and Dad continued with his alcohol. I got caught up with my friends running around, getting high and goofing off, but I still was responsible and kept my job and went to work in order to contribute with expenses at home. Cheche had gotten way out of control. He had been sticking up people at gunpoint, taking their money, jewelry, and anything worth value as he had been doing all along, but this time it was much worst then before. My parents argued a lot because of him and were at each other's throat daily. Cheche had gotten too dangerous and did not fear anyone. We all loved him, but kept a bit distance from him. While he stayed at home with us, we fellowshiped with him but went about our own business. I sure didn't want any part of what he was doing, and neither did brother Kato. Kato had been doing some things that were wrong, but he too kept a certain distance from our brother. Both Cheche and Kato clashed at times, and Kato knew Cheche wasn't one to mess with, especially when Cheche was under the influence of drugs. Kato wasn't afraid of Cheche, but Kato knew Cheche to be extremely dangerous and would have done anything crazy had he tried anything against him. Cheche committed many atrocities and he was to be feared. Drugs had completely taken over his life, and he did not care what he did and who he hurt. I was no angel, but I kept a good head on my shoulders. I loved my parties and dances, especially at nightclubs. The Latin Hustle was what I enjoyed dancing to, but my favorite was the Latin Salsa dances. All these things were some of the things that continued to happen at home, and things were really getting unbearable for my parents to handle.

-18-

ANNE'S BROKEN MARRIAGE

As things at home were spiraling out of control, one day, my youngest sister Anne and her husband separated in the heat of the moment. They engaged into this huge argument, and as things escalated between them, he grabbed all his things and walked out of the house on Anne, leaving her behind as if that were okay to do. He walked away from all his responsibilities and duties to love and to protect Anne until death do them apart. That day he broke all his marriage vows to Anne. I was sitting on the front porch of the house as he was walking out. As he walked away, he mumbled some words out of his mouth, looked back, and kept walking saying, "I'm out of here." He never returned for my sister, and it was the last time we ever saw or heard from him.

I'm not sure what exactly they had been arguing about, but my sister needed her privacy and their own place, and that added to their problems. They were only staying with us temporarily until they were able to get back on their feet, but unfortunately, this turn of events changed everything for Anne, and she found herself single without her husband and pregnant with their first unborn child.

Walking out on Anne was extremely devastating to her. Whatever happened to the marriage vows "for better or for worse" and/or until death do us part"? I'm not saying marriage is perfect because we all can make stupid mistakes, sin, and mess things up, (it's happened to me), but God in his word hates divorce and abhors it. His will for every married couple is for them to work things out and stay together as long as there isn't any physical or mental abuse or sexual immorality (Matthew 19:3-9). Each marriage has to joined-together and work things out. In a marriage, we need to strive to get along, communicate, prosper, respect one another, and love one another fervently. Paul had even written about these delicate matters in the New Testament (Ephesians 5:25–33).

It wasn't easy on Anne being pregnant and trying to cope with everything that was going on around her life. After years had gone by, they finalized their divorce, and their son waited until he was in his early thirties before meeting his biological father.

It was such a difficult time for my sister after her spouse ran out on her, but she survived.

After Anne's husband abandoned her, she started having major problems with Dad again. He was always on her case for no real reason at all. He always had something to say to her, and it wasn't nice. He reproached Anne and didn't even care that she was pregnant, going through her own drama, with her husband abandoning her and feeling stranded without any money or the proper resources to move on with her life.

Things at home had been escalating and mounting for the worse. As these things had been happening, Anne finally decided that it was time to leave home, and away from Dad. In fact, if my recollection serves me right, I think Dad asked her to pack her things and leave the house (he kicked her out). Anne took courage and left the house and went to live temporary with a relative until she was able to get herself on her own feet. Occasionally, I took time out of my schedule to visit her, just to make sure that she was okay.

As time went by, Anne finally was able to rent her own place toward the south end of Broad Street in Newark. This was Anne's very first apartment as a single mother, and though she struggled with paying the bills, somehow she managed. By this time, she already had given birth to her first child, a beautiful baby boy with blue eyes, and he brought joy to her life. She finally felt a sense of peace and freedom in her life. It was a new beginning for her, but as a single mother and having to raise a child all on her own, things didn't come by easy for her. Here's a recap on her marriage.

She was glowing from cheek to cheek and wore a beautiful white wedding gown and looked amazingly beautiful. She was super excited the day of her wedding, but also was a nervous wreck making preparations. Those of us that have legally married in a church know how stressful that can be, but once the wedding vows and the ceremonial take place, the storm calms down, and tranquility sets in. It was a very special moment in her life that day. It was the day that Prince Charming swept her off her feet and made her feel like a queen. What a happy moment it was for her. They had gotten married at a Baptist church, but celebrated their wedding at St. Thomas Catholic Church on Ludlow Street, Newark, New Jersey. The church was part of OKH Community right across the projects.

-19-

CHECHE'S IMPRISONMENT

With all that had been going on at home, Cheche's drug habit continued to worsen. He was completely out of control, and something had to be done fast. He's burdened my parents, causing them lots of pain, much problems, and Mom couldn't stop worrying about him. The only time she felt at ease was when he came home to sleep. He had Dad on edge all the time. He continued to assault others as the opportunities came by. The more drugs he consumed, the more his need was to get out late at night and victimize his next target. The authorities were pursuing him, but he didn't care a bit about that. He put many lives at risk, including himself. This was the worse we had ever seen him. It was so bad we all started getting concerned for his life. Some of us tried talking sense into him, and though he knew we were right and that we were just trying to help, he nixed everything off. Things with Cheche were never the same due to his drug addiction. By this time, Satan had taken full control of Cheche's mind. Only a miracle from God would change his situation. He had been shooting dope a few times a day, barely eating much of anything. Dope became his life, and he could no longer live without it. It was horrible to see him like this.

My other siblings went through some of the same things as he did, just not as bad. But this was Cheche's condition all day long until he got into bed. In the mornings, after his showers and a little breakfast, he locked himself in the bathroom for about thirty minutes or more, inject himself, and out to the streets to do his thing.

As the authorities continued their search for him, you would think that he would slow things down and try to control a bit his situation, but that was never the case. If anything, he armed himself with guns and continued committing crimes at gunpoint—all this just to get a fix. The authorities kept stopping by to inform us that something had to be done before he ended up dead or hurting someone. They even stressed the possibility that any forceful confrontation with the authorities may turn out deadly unless he surrendered.

Unfortunately, someone had to give him up, but who? Who would have the courage and the will power to hand him over to the authorities? Nobody at home really wanted to spill the beans on him, but someone had to do something really fast, before it was too late, and he end-up in the grave.

One beautiful hot sunny day around noon, Dad walks in from the outdoors and goes directly upstairs to the second floor and entered my room where Cheche had been sleeping. When Dad saw that Cheche was still in bed, he woke him up, screaming his lungs out at him, and demanded he get his rear end out of bed and go find himself a job. That was the biggest mistake my father had ever done with Cheche. My dad did not yet grasp how dangerous Cheche had become, and to do something of this sort to a dangerous being, it's a big no-no. I couldn't blame my dad for being so upset, and he was in his rightful place to demand that Cheche get out of bed, but it almost costs Dad his life. The least Cheche could have done, was show him some respect, but this wasn't the case.

There are certain things in life that sons should never do and Cheche crossed the line. All hell broke loose that day, and when Dad woke Cheche from his sleep and demanded he get up and out of the house, Cheche got out of bed, put his pajama robe on, and grabbed his gun then approached Dad and threatened his life with it. This was a side of Cheche my father had never seen. This made Dad tremble, and for the first time, it made him fear my brother. Cheche threatened Dad in such a way that Dad never again got in his face. Cheche pointed the gun at him and told him that he would use it on him and blow his brains out. Fear struck at the core of Dad's heart, and he immediately went into his bedroom while Cheche was still shouting threats at him. It was terrifying to see what had just developed between Dad and Cheche. Cheche never really wanted to threaten Dad, but he too had had enough of Dad from all the years of Dad's mental abuse not only toward him but toward Mom as well. Cheche loved Mom so much that he would have killed for her safety. Even so, when I saw how things turned out that day, I determined to be the one to hand Cheche over to the authorities. I knew that if I didn't do something, Cheche would have probably ended up hurting Dad badly or shooting him down with his gun. I couldn't take that chance, and though I didn't want to be the one to turn him in, he left me no choice. Moses wrote in the Old Testament, "Honor your father and your mother, so that you may live long in the land the Lord your God is giving you" (Exodus 20:12, NIV).

To avoid any other dreadful disasters from occurring at home, I had to move quickly and take action. I couldn't in my conscious allow any harm to come to both my father and brother. This would have devastated my mother and the family, and I wasn't about to allow any of this to happen. After everything calmed down and cooled off, I quietly walked out of the house and spoke with Kato who was standing outside the front porch, asking what had just happened. He was just coming from his girlfriend's place. I gave him the latest news and what I had planned to do, in order to avoid a tragedy from happening. Kato agreed that it was for the best. In fact, he said he was thinking to do the same. This wasn't something to take lightly, and we knew it was either now or never. Despite Kato's mishaps with dad, he stilled love Dad and was actually concerned for his well being. We knew things were at stake with Cheche, and if another incident of this sort would have occurred, no doubt Cheche would have killed Dad in the heat of the moment. In the past, before this incident, both Kato and I had our shares of unpleasant moments with Cheche, so we knew how dangerous he had gotten. After Kato agreed with me that it was for the best to turn him in, I pressed forward and called the authorities, but set conditions with the authorities before they came out to arrest him.

The authorities needed concrete evidence to keep Cheche behind bars without bail, and since I knew some concrete information, I provided the authorities with the information they needed in order to come out for his arrest. They agreed to my terms, and after verifying the information I gave them was concrete, early the next morning, they came out quietly, and arrested him. These were my terms: (1) they were not to blow their sirens and make a scene outside the perimeter of our property; (2) they were to enter the house quietly without alarming my parents; (3) they would never to reveal to my brother that indeed it was I who turned him in; (4) under any circumstances they were not to harm my brother; (5) they were to gently get him out of bed and give him the chance to get dressed appropriately, allow him to brush his teeth, and then place their handcuffs on him and gently walk him out of the house to their patrol car without making a scene.

This was the hardest thing I ever had to do. It literally broke my heart to have to be the one to turn him in, but he left me no choice. Mom was in tears, but she knew his life was just speared. Everyone was sad that day as Cheche was finally apprehended and taken away in the patrol car. Do I have any regrets, the answer to that is no. Why? "Because I literally saved the lives of both my father and my brother." This was something I never thought I would ever have to do. But desperate times call for desperate measures. Under no circumstances would I have ever allowed such a tragedy from happening.

Otherwise, I would have lived to regret this day for the rest of my life. As I write their stories my family's story, I can't help getting emotional as tears drenched my eyes and shed down my face, remembering every single detail as it all happened. I always went out of my way to visit him behind bars. Cheche was sentenced to Rahway Prison for approximately five years without parole. I saved my family from further hardship. After his arrest, a burden was lifted off my parents' shoulders with a big sigh of relief. By God's grace, I delivered Dad and Cheche from the enemy's hand and brought a little peace to our parents. They knew he was better off in prison.

Kato was relieved to see Cheche go behind bars, and with good reason. Kato was upset at him for forcing himself on one of his ex-girlfriends. He wanted to get back at him for what happened with his ex-girlfriend, so when Cheche was incarcerated, Kato felt a sigh of relief. He wasn't happy that Cheche was behind bars, but it helped prevent a tragedy between them.

-20-

MY PARENTS SEPARATE

After Cheche had been incarcerated, things at home cooled off a bit, but my parents were still having major problems. Every day Dad continued drinking his booze and it got to be way too much.

Mom was no longer drinking. She had completely stopped because she didn't like how it was making her feel and what it had been doing to Dad. Dad continued, and at this point in his life, he was a full-blown alcoholic. Dad wasn't always an alcoholic. He was hardworking and provided for the family. I admit he was a good provider and a good father and had put up with a lot of things at home with my older siblings. When he worked, he didn't drink booze all the time. He was very responsible and took care of his family well. But whatever happened to us living at the house in Paterson changed everything in our lives. It was in Paterson that Dad started drinking more frequently and going to the bars. He slowly started changing, and my siblings were always getting in some kind of trouble. It was sad to see how our beautiful family fell apart and divided among ourselves. Satan had taken over our lives, and things gradually turned for the worse.

I was twenty-one when Mom finally left Dad. The story goes as follows: As usual, Mom arrived in from work, greeted me and my friend as we were sitting out on the front porch; it was nice and sunny on a hot afternoon day. As she opens the screen door and enters the house (the main door was opened), Dad immediately went into a rage and shouted at her saying, "It is late, where the heck have you been and why are you so late coming in from your job?" His friends were home with him, and they all had been drinking and gotten drunk. Mom was only about thirty to forty minutes late. Mom didn't drive a car, so she always had to take a bus ride, back and forth to work and home. That day, she either missed the bus, and/or if my memory serves me right, the bus was delayed, causing her to wait longer at the bus stop. As Mom attempted to explain her situation, Dad completely cut her off and humiliated her. He used obscene words and started name-calling her, things which I dare not say or use in this book—use your imagination. That was Dad's biggest mistake ever, and he lived to regret it.

I was there present and can testify that indeed, this is the true story as it happened. Dad should have never treated Mom that way. Mom was so happy that day being that it was a Friday, and with the weekend coming up.. She was exhausted, tired, hungry, and was about to get ready to cook for Dad and the family, to then go and relax. But Dad went off on her leaving her no other option but to walk out and leave. Dad had slammed mom with his abusive language, they exchanged a few words, and Mom immediately made a U-turn and walked right back out the front door, and down the porch stairs, then said to me, "she was leaving him for good, and not to ever expect for her to return home, and that she'll be staying at her sibling's house." As she walked away, Dad suddenly rages out the front door and from the porch called out to her using horrific names, attracting the attention of the entire neighborhood; mom was halfway down the block by this time. It was horrible. Mom finally got the courage to walk away from it all. She never came back and Dad found himself without his wife of twenty-eight years.

I was in complete disbelief, and didn't think Mom had it in her, but she surprised us all. I guess enough was enough. I remembered Lulu and Kato stopping by right after it all went down, but by this time, mom was long gone, and Dad was still on the front porch drunk, and cursing as if mom was still there. My friend was sitting on the porch across from me, and he couldn't believe what had just happened. We were all taken by surprise. The whole neighborhood was in shock. They heard everything and watched as things were unfolding. Dad thought she would eventually return, but as each day went by, Mom was nowhere to be found and Dad's concerns mounted. Every day he pounded me with questions about Mom's whereabouts, to the point that he started accusing me of harboring infidelity and that Mom was a—use your imagination. It started getting to him until it finally sunk in that she wasn't returning to him. Mom had more guts then any one ever thought or ever given her credit for. She wasn't going to turn into a pillar of salt, like Lot's wife in the Bible (Genesis 19:26). She kept walking forward, never looked back, and Dad never saw Mom again. Dad found himself at a loss without Mom. What a sad ending for my parents. It was a sad moment for all of us. Mom had always promised us that one day she would leave Dad, but that it would be after we all (my siblings and I) would reached adulthood. Her promised was fulfilled, and it was a day never to forget. Was Dad a bad person? No, he was a very nice man and got along well with family and friends. But his booze got in the way of his priorities and of everything else that matter.

After my parents' separation, I felt the need to stay home and look after Dad. I didn't want to abandon him especially now, when he needed me the most. He was vulnerable, and anyone could have stopped by the house to harm him, especially those that knew he was alone in the house while I was at work and everyone else was long gone, though Kato was nearby. I worked the first shift, so there was no way I could be there to watch him until I got home in the afternoons. I still had the need to spend time with friends, but I made sure that he was okay before going out. His alcoholic friends where there with him during the daytime hours, so I knew to keep a close watch on him and on his friends, and made sure no harm came to him. His friends couldn't be trusted, so I made sure they each knew that I had my eyes on them. They were only there to get drunk and to see how they can get some of his cash. Kato often stopped by the house and checked on Dad as well. It may not have seemed like it to Dad, but Kato and I had his back, and we weren't going to allow anyone to harm him in any form or way.

Unfortunately, Dad continued drinking and didn't like too much that I was still at home watching over his shoulder. It was hard communicating with him, and instead of appreciating me being there with him, he was reproachful toward me, constantly nagging me about Mom. It was heart-breaking to see Dad in the condition he was, but he was far too gone by this time and upset at everyone for all that went down. What he needed was a miracle from God. Dad had become impossible to live with, and after about a week or two had gone by since Mom had left, he demanded I leave the house and go live on my own. I couldn't believe what I was hearing, but it didn't take me by surprise. He asked me to leave because I didn't appreciate the ugly things he would say to me about Mom. I asked him not to talk about Mom that way to me, especially in front of his friends, but that only angered him more so he kicked me out of the house, he demanded violently telling me to get the heck out and find my own place to live. I felt really bad for him, but I knew it was best to leave and get my own place and move on with my life.

As I was walking out of the house, as always, Kato was approaching the house to see how things were at home, and I informed him of what had just taken place and asked him to accompany me to see if I can find myself a place to live. He immediately tagged along, and after we walked down to Broadway

Avenue and got like a quarter of a block away, we spotted a private house with a furnished room for rent. It was less than a five-minute walk from home on Delavan Avenue. I met with the owner and rented the room on the third floor and then headed back home with Kato who then helped me bring my personal things back to the apartment. Within an hour, I was completely gone out of my parents' house and left Dad to be on his own with his friends. Kato went his way after helping me, and I stayed in to unpack my things at my rental. I felt a sigh of relief and felt good I had my own place, but I felt sad for Dad. He had gone completely mad. Now he was completely on his own to do as he wish, drenched in booze with anger blowing out of the top of his ears. Dad had his youngest sister who occasionally would stop by the house to look after him and took him cooked meals. She lived about five minutes north of us.

Once I left to be on my own, I never looked back and made my own life. I was still twenty-one during this time, and since I had a good job, I managed well. From my apartment window on Broadway, I can still see Dad hanging out in front of the liquor store on Broadway Avenue with his buddies having a drink or two. The liquor store was across the street from where I was renting. Many times I stepped out and approached Dad just to see how he was, but the conversations were short. Other than that, I stayed completely away from the house. If it wasn't for God, who knows where I be today? Only God knows!

The truth was that I never agreed with Mom leaving Dad, but I clearly understood that she was tired of all the nonsense that went on. A woman could only handle but so much before a husband presses all the wrong buttons. I give her credit for not abandoning us when we were young. I tip my hats off to Mom for being the greatest mother in the world. The fact that she never abandoned us while we were still young, truly showed how much she really care for each and every one of us.

The Holy Scriptures tells us that women are the weaker vessel in a marriage. We husbands are to treat them with love and respect. We should never treat our wives' as if they are insignificant. For those of us who have wives, God gave them to us to be our helpers and our equals. Treating them any less would be considered ungodly and sinful (1 Peter 3:7).

Dad left his emotional scars behind, but we all got over them with God's help. God is great, and we must forgive!

After Mom and Anne were gone from the house, I'd visit each of them as I had promised them. It didn't take Mom too much time to get her own apartment. My maternal grandmother before leaving for Puerto Rico, transferred her apartment over to Mom at the Seth Boyden Housing Authority. Mom still had some siblings living there with their families, and that helped her to cope with everything that had been going on.

I never held resentments toward Dad, knowing he had a drinking problem. Dealing with my older siblings was never an easy thing for him. It put him under lots of stress, and it contributed to the way he treated us. Despite everything that happened, I loved him and forgave him. His youngest sister and her husband helped him until he was able to sell the house and move to Puerto Rico. I think that if it wasn't for them, Dad would have probably been found dead all alone in the house. I thank God they kept him sane and came to his rescue. Ending a marriage and losing all your love ones has to be one of the hardest thing any couple has to face. I don't wish that on anyone.

It may take a whole lifetime to establish a relationship and a family, but it'll take seconds and minutes for Satan to destroy it (John 10:10). The good news is that Jesus is the answer to all our problems.

-21-

LIVING ON MY OWN

After moving out to my own apartment, I felt as free as a bird, flying around the skies—like a free man. I started enjoying life to the fullest like never before. It felt great to live independently, away from my parents and from all the chaos that surrounded my life at home with the family. I had a good-paying job at a nearby hardware store, and it was about a ten- to fifteen-minute walk from my place. I worked hard, and things started moving along my way. It was a new beginning for me and it was the best thing I had done in a long time.

Occasionally, I would run into some of my friends from the projects and from around the corner on Delavan Avenue. I never forgot any of my friends, and whenever I had spare time, I went out of my way to visit them. I appreciated all my friends, but I had a job, and I couldn't spend too much time out there like in the past. Being streetwise taught me a lot of things. I learned survival skills and wasn't afraid to work. Work never killed anybody, and since I love making money, I was devoted to my job and did my best to stay out of trouble. I did well for myself and my whole life was changing. It was here in this apartment where I learned to dance salsa and disco and got really good at it.

While I was living at my parents' house, I had only been working part-time making only $80 a week, but after I rented my own apartment, I spoke with my employer and he agreed to raised my salary wages to a full-time forty-hour week. I had a good work ethic, and my employer loved the way I worked, and the Lord put his grace upon me.

Friday and Saturday nights, I hung out at some of the best nightclubs in New Jersey. I met many beautiful women and dated at every opportunity. I loved having mixed drinks and a Heineken, but I did my best to keep it together. I didn't like being drunk or having any hangovers on the following day, though it did happened a few times.

Dancing truly became part of my life and gave me a sense of belonging. I learned lots of dancing techniques and quickly learned that women love guys that can dance. It was as if a new door had opened for me. As my dancing skills advanced, so did the women in my life. Everywhere I went, women wanted to dance with me, and I loved every moment of it. This was a new hobby in my life, and I wasn't about to let it go. I was just getting started. I became a true womanizer and the opportunities were endless. I gave a few private lessons to women that interest me, but my interest was more than that. These women became my lovers. Dancing gave me the opportunity to date women of all walks of life.

There wasn't a nightclub where I wasn't well known. New York was famous for having the best live Salsa Latin Bands. I love going out to El Corso, and it was located on East Eighty-Sixth Street in Manhattan. I introduced my sister Lulu to this nightclub, and after a while, she and I went there for weeks on: Thursdays, Fridays, and Saturday nights. We met many new friends and became regulars there and Lulu and I had much fun together.

I loved exercising and looking sharp all the time. I never left the house without wearing my cologne and I liked being clean-cut and clean-shaved with money in my pocket.

I was finally living my life the way I always wanted to live it. The ladies didn't mind having me around, and I enjoyed their company. I truly was my father's son. They say the apple doesn't fall far from the tree. There was no doubt I had his gene in me, and just like he was, I too had become a big flirt.

Living on my own taught me the fundamentals of life. I matured quickly and took care of my responsibilities. Working also taught me that as long as I worked, I can have and do whatsoever I wanted. I learned that having money in my pocket and working hard for it gave me the opportunity to prosper and get ahead in life. I didn't like freeloading off anybody, and I couldn't stand lazy people; I hated them. I even worked on Saturdays and did that for three years without ever missing a Saturday of work. I became a better man.

I learned in life that I can do anything I put my heart to do. This was a victory for me. My life started changing, and although I was still out there smoking weed and getting high with my friends, things were changing for me.

During the course of time, Anne needed to find a more affordable place to live in, for her and her toddler, so I got her a furnished room in the same house I was living in, right across from my apartment on the third floor, door-to-door to me. There were just two furnished rooms on the third floor, so we had the floor for ourselves. It seemed that I was always her guardian angel and she felt safe being there with me. She stayed there for some time and later on move back to Delavan Avenue to a bigger apartment with the man who's now her husband; we knew him from Delavan Avenue. Shortly after she left, I packed my bags and left for Puerto Rico.

-22-

LEAVING FOR PUERTO RICO

I left for Puerto Rico when I was around twenty-three. My brother-in-law was on the same flight with me and a friend of his, so we took the same cab together with a friend and they dropped me off first, and after about an hour, they left to their destination. Once there, I had much fun with my mother's families and enjoy life there as if I were on a long vacation. After two months in Puerto Rico, I was faced with the problem of not finding work.

Employment did not come by easy for me, especially because I was an outsider without any real education at the time. I had depleted all my funds, so I knew that the only right thing to do was to pack up my luggage and return back to New Jersey. I never liked freeloading off anybody, especially from my own families. I had been staying with my maternal grandmother and not being able to contribute financially was what forced me to leave. Had it not been for that, I would have stayed living in Puerto Rico. Puerto Rico was beautiful, the people there were humble, kind, and they treated me with love. My grandmother was always attentive to my needs, and whatever I needed, she provided me with. My relatives and I always sat in the front porch with her and chatted for hours on in. My grandmother was religious and loved telling us stories about God. She used to tell me that God was going to return to earth for his people on a Saturday night. I don't know why she always said that, but I believed it and so did everyone else. After all, she was Grandma, and when she spoke, everyone listened. I don't know what day of the week God is returning for us, but the point of her story was that one day he will return. Grandma was strict, but in a very sweet loving way. Her house sat on a hill above the ocean view. My cousins and I loved hearing her stories especially when she made us laugh. She was kind of funny. About ten years after my departure from Puerto Rico, the Lord took Grandma home to be with him. She was loved by everyone.

Prior to my tenure in Puerto Rico at Grandma's place, I hadn't been there since Dad took me away from there when I was eleven living with my father's family. While I was there living with grandma, I visited my father's family only once or twice. Other than that, I was too busy doing my own thing. Years had gone by, and things were different for me, and I just wanted to spend time with my other relatives since I hadn't seen them since they had left New Jersey, and they were the ones I grew up with. We had a lot of catching up to do, and that's exactly what we did.

It was great being in Puerto Rico and spending quality time with my mother's family, but all good things must come to an end. When I decided to leave, one of my dear cousins came back with me to the States. We were best of friends and very close cousins. We had practically been raised together back in the Dayton Street projects.

Before returning to the States, it happened one day that while looking out the window from my friend's house who lived along one of the side streets of the plaza square, I suddenly saw my dad walking, so I ran down to greet him. I asked him where was he going," and he said, "To the liquor store." I tried convincing him to allow me to walk him back to his car and have him return to his home in Quebrada which was in the county of Camuy. He was drunk and I thought he had enough as it was. He then asked me, "What on earth are you doing here?"

And I said, "I'm with some cousins visiting friends."

He scolded me, mumble-jumbled a few words at me and went about his business. He was stoned drunk out of his mind, and it seemed that nothing had changed with him. I felt horrible for him wishing there was something else I can do, but he never allowed it. It saddened my heart to see him drunk and suffering, but there was nothing anyone can do. His family in Puerto Rico loved him dearly, and tried helping him for a while, but he kept running back to the bottle. Unfortunately, drinking was the only method he used to cope with his problems.

It was the last time I saw my dad alive.

-23-

BACK IN NEW JERSEY

Once I was back in New Jersey, Anne let me crashed in her place, until I was able to get back on my own two feet. Anne was always kind to me, and enjoyed having me around. My former employer rehired me, and within a month or so, I rented the same furnished apartment I had on Broadway. I was grateful to Anne for allowing me the allotted time I needed to stay with her, but now it was time for me to move on and take charge of my life again. Anne was a sweetheart and had a heart of gold, and I shall always be grateful to her.

While working at my former place of employment, I returned to school and pursued my education. I had been a high school dropout just like my siblings had done before me, and decided I needed to rectify some of my past mistakes. Per my request, my employer allowed me to work half days in the afternoons, so that I can further pursuit my education fulltime during the day, and I earned my high school diploma and a business administration diploma (although, I had to re-do my high school diploma years later, due to an error). After completing my studies, my employer allowed me to return to work fulltime with a better pay and more responsibilities.

My work ethics improved and a wide door of opportunities opened wide for me. It goes to show us that it's never too late to do something about our situations, and we can fix and rectify past mistakes. At the end of it all, it paid off, and my life changed for the better.

I was nightclubbing, dancing, drinking, socializing, and having the time of my life. During the day I worked, and during the night I partied. Although I worked six days a week from Mondays through Saturdays, my weekends started on Thursdays through Sundays. Mondays through Wednesdays I hung out with friends, and had a good time as well.

I did whatever I wanted to do and whatever pleased me. I was king of my own castle and it felt great.

I dressed to kill—sharp looking—and I loved flashing my shoes and my big hats around. I always felt that a man who dressed nice and can afford wearing expensive shoes should also be a man that can afford having the prettiest looking ladies around him. Maybe that wasn't true for every man out there, but for me, it was like walking with diamonds shoelaces. We all know that diamonds are a girls' best friend. Well, I was that diamond, and I attracted women like if I wore a gigantic magnet around my neck down to my waistline. This was a recap of my former lifestyle, but is not who I am today.

DANGERS WITHIN

One time, a man I knew who had been renting an apartment in the same private house I was living in asked me to come in his apartment to drink some beer with him. I didn't think anything of it and thought he was just being a friendly neighbor, so I went inside his apartment with him; he lived on the second floor. As I sat and started drinking the beer, I suddenly started blacking out and immediately realized his evil intentions toward me. He drugged the beer I had been drinking. The drug literally paralyzed me to the point that I can barely move. Somehow I found the strength to get up off the chair and walked toward the door to exit his apartment, and as soon as I opened the door, I felled flat on my face. I had loss all my strength and blacked out. Had it not been for another neighbor who had been walking up the stairs at that very moment and saw I had been drugged and fallen as I was exiting the man's apartment, I promise, that today I probably would have not been the man I am today. If I had to live through something of this nature, I don't think I could have lived a normal life. I didn't know God back then or much about his love toward me, but God had been watching out for me. I believe God had sent my other neighbor to rescue me that day because if he hadn't, who knows where would I have been today. I probably would have been abused sexually, and/or, even murdered—only God knows. God has been a merciful God to me. He has loved me unconditionally. For sure I'm undeserving of his love. If you have been victimized by these kind of men, it doesn't mean God doesn't love you, caused he really does, and no matter what's ever happened in your life, his love for you is deeper then the oceans and higher than the heavens. Give him a chance to show you his love!

MY CONVERSION TO CHRISTIANITY

That's how I was back in the day until the Spirit of the Lord started working in my life. It all began on September of 1983, after moving in with my sister Mary and her husband at their apartment in Elizabeth. Mary had recently remarried and she and her husband were attending church. She was off the streets and had cleaned herself up, trying to recuperate her life again. I was twenty-five, and Cheche had recently been released from prison after serving his five year sentence, and went to live with a girlfriend of his in Newark. Mary and her husband invited me to church with them one Saturday night, and my life was never the same after that. As I surrendered my life to Christ, everything started changing. I no longer had the desire to show off my shoes or what I wore. All the gold chains and expensive rings I wore on my hands didn't mean a thing to me anymore. The Holy Spirit was dealing heavy on my heart about these things, that it was all vanity. I still enjoy looking and dressing sharp, but this time, it wasn't too much for the ladies; it was for Christ. In no way I am exaggerating. Jesus changed my heart, and after he did that, he also started changing my thinking. In the Old Testament, the prophet Isaiah writes, "For my thoughts are not your thoughts, neither are your ways my ways, " declares the Lord. "As the heavens are higher than the earth, so are my ways higher than your ways and my thoughts than your thoughts" (Isaiah 55:8–9, NIV).

I no longer was thinking of partying with the ladies, dating and/or going out to nightclubs. Instead, I was thinking on how to please the Almighty God. It was no longer about me, but about Jesus and for Jesus. I just couldn't get enough of Jesus. Jesus was the best thing that ever happened to me, especially, at a time when I most needed him. He saved my poor, wretched soul and eradicated all the wrong things I had been doing. Jesus is everything to me, and he's my Lord and I intend to keep him that way.

Prior to my conversion, I shagged in a few times with a few ladies that I had been dating. "Shag" is a British term for "shacking up," which is a term we use for living together as fornicators, without being legally married. Satan had me bound to this kind of life and planned on destroying the rest of my life, but God had a different purpose for me. God snatched me away from Satan's gripped claws. Christ then broke all the strongholds the devil had over me when I gave my heart to God. God is bigger, stronger, and smarter than Satan, and in Christ we have victory over the devil. My life is covered with the blood of Jesus (1 John 1:7), and God keeps his protection over me.

Almost immediately after giving my heart to Christ, the Lord started dealing with me and moving in my life powerfully. I was on a spiritual rampage, and everywhere I went, I preached at every opportunity given to me and won many souls for Christ. The devil started hating me even more. He didn't know what else to do with me, and I resisted him, causing him to flee from me in Jesus Christ name. Every time I mentioned the name of Jesus or the blood of Jesus Christ, Satan and his demons trembled and left the scene (James 4:7). I was getting stronger in the Lord, I started attending church services on weekends, and started taking time out to do my homework at home. What homework, you might ask? My response to you is, the reading and the studying of the Holy Scriptures. Every day, I made it my business to read God's word, and as I spent countless hours reading his book, I found tremendous fulfillment in his word. His book is alive, and it is the living word of God. It is the only book in the world that has been written thousands of years ago, and yet it contains life and salvation in its context. Either we believe in him and accept Jesus Christ as our personal Lord and savior, or we can reject him and stand condemned forever (John 3:18).

After I left Newark and moved in with Mary to Elizabeth, my life as a Christian took off, and I was on fire for Jesus. After my first year in church, I got involved with the music. I learned to be submissive to church authority like never before. This is something that many church members are still struggling with today and have declined to obey God in this area. Shame on them because one day soon, God will call them to account, and they will have to answer to him. This was all new to me, but I knew I was in the right place seeking after God's heart. The rest of my older siblings were still messing around, and during this time, Kato had gone to Puerto Rico to live for a while. I'm not sure why he had gotten incarcerated over there, but he did before coming back to the States. My siblings were still doing their usual thing, spending their lives in and out of jail and still committing crimes throughout the City of Newark and Elizabeth. This had become the norm for them. All throughout my years, since I was about eleven or twelve, I was in and out of jails visiting my siblings. A few times Satan tried to have me killed, but was unsuccessful.

God was watching out for me from his heavenly throne, and I didn't even know it. When I think of all that had been happening in my life, for sure I must have had the Lord's angels going crazy, chasing me around just to protect me from harm's way (Hebrews 1:14).

Satan thought he had me, and for a time there he actually did, but thank God for Jesus who delivered me from the satanic yokes that had me bound to the works of Satan. There's no doubt that Christ had been interceding for me at the right hand of the Father (Romans 8:34).

Mary's son Tony was still a young lad, but he was a good boy. By this time, I was no longer working at the hardware store on Broadway, but had got me another job on Market Street, downtown Newark working for a furniture store. Moving to Elizabeth was the best decision of my life after giving my heart to Christ because it gave me a chance at a brand new start. I left all my Newark friends behind and met a bunch of new church friends that helped me grow in the Lord. This was exactly what I needed in my life. Sometimes we have to move away far from everything we know in order to start a new life fresh with God and have new beginnings. I was becoming a different man—a new man. My friends back in Newark could not believe how I had been changing, especially the ladies; they were flabbergasted. Nothing else mattered to me. I was a new man in Christ, and I loved the changes that were happening to my life. I was happy, and I didn't need any weed to fulfill my needs or any sex with the ladies to get my free thrills. Indeed, I was a new changed man in Christ!

My old lifestyle was passing away while Christ was cleansing my spirit, soul and body (1 Thessalonians 5:23). The joy of the Lord that I was experiencing was amazing. Let me tell you, feeling God's presence in my life was the most wonderful experienced I've ever had happened to me. It was a high that no drug can give.

The only side effects it leaves us with is love, joy, and happiness. With all that in mind, I didn't need anything else. I was satisfied knowing that I was in God's hands and that all the wrong I had ever done was now all forgiven and gone for good.

My life was being sanctified by the Holy Spirit because I was finally obeying the Lord (1 Corinthians 6:9-11). My Creator had all my attention, and he was pleased with me and poured his grace upon me. I was truly a born-again Christian man (John 3:3–8). No more religion. I wasn't religious before my conversion to Christianity, but I pertained to a religion and only once or twice a year I went to church (I had stopped going to church after I was about sixteen). The differences between both religions were just that: One was nothing but a religion, and the other offered me salvation. The scriptures indicate that there's only one faith, my friends (Ephesians 4:4-6). While all this had been happening to me, Kato had been committing crimes in Puerto Rico and was prosecuted and sent to one of Puerto Rico's prisons; probably in San Juan.

CHECHE'S APPEARANCE AND REDEMPTION

Meanwhile, I was working at the furniture store on Market Street in Newark, and my brother Cheche was passing by on foot. Now he didn't know I was working in the area of downtown Newark and didn't see me, because I was inside the store, and he didn't look through the glass windows as he walked by, but I saw him. He kept walking and went about his business.

When I saw him, my heart literally wanted to break in pieces. As I kept glancing at him from inside the store window, horror struck my heart. He looked so horribly sick as if he had a horrible disease. It crushed my heart to see him that way. After seeing him like that, I could no longer stay still at work, and I couldn't wait to get home to talk to my sister Mary and her husband that we needed to bring him home immediately to help him out before he would end up dead somewhere in the streets. His condition was so bad that it literally caused my heart to beat in patient.

At the first glance, I knew he had AIDS. His face was sunk in, and he was really skinny from all the drugs he had been injecting in his body. Prior to this, I hadn't seen him for a good while. I had never seen him so skinny like this before; he looked like a zombie with the face of a skeleton. I saw the face of death in him like never before, and now that I knew the Lord, I knew to act immediately before Satan would put him to death. After arriving home from work and expressing my immediate concerns for Cheche's life, Mary and her husband agreed that we needed to go find him and bring him home as soon as possible. The very next morning, we went out and found him staying up in an apartment on Orange Street in Newark with a girlfriend of his at the time. We spoke with him, he agreed to come with us, and we brought him home to stay with us. He had needle marks up and down his arms and over other areas of his body. I was so worried for him I couldn't even sleep at night We were not afraid that he had AIDS. We still loved him, fed him, bathed him, and clothed him. He was too weak to do any of these things. We prayed for him every day, and the very first weekend that came up, we took him to church with us, and he gave his heart to Jesus Christ. We knew that his days were counted and that he had but little time left before death came to him. So you can imagine the joy that overcame us as he stood there in front of the altar and gave his heart to Christ; it overwhelmed us. Oh, what a merciful God we have. We were the instruments the Holy Spirit used to bring him to the light of God. Had we left him to be, he would have never made it to heaven. The drugs had finally taken a toll on him, and his body could no longer handle the abuse anymore. It sent chills of my spine. He literally looked like a skeleton. It was hard to even look at him, even scary, but we didn't care. The time he spent with us during those last days made him very happy. He was such a handsome young man, well-structured, and to see what drugs had done to him, was the unimaginable. It destroyed his health completely and left him sucked dried.

During the time he was at home with us, we gradually helped him get off the drugs, but it wasn't easy at all. He went through tough withdrawals and that's the worst thing any hard-core junkie addicted to drugs can possibly go through. It was hard to see him in so much pain, and all we can do was give him words of encouragement. He revealed to us that he no longer was shooting dope to get high but to help him with the horrible pains he was feeling in his body. His body was immune to the drugs, and he no longer was feeling the effects of the drugs as he did in the past. It was heartbreaking and saddened all our hearts. It was a very serious situation, and he needed medical attention. We all knew that unless God were to do some kind of miracle, his chances for survival were slim to none. We also knew that it was just a matter of time before he would go home to be with the Lord. If anything, he had but a few weeks to live and it was during the cold winter months of November and December of 1983. During the month of December, my family and I received bad news from Puerto Rico that our father died, so I made arrangements to travel by myself to Puerto Rico for the funeral arrangements. I was the only sibling flying out for my father's death, with the exception that Kato was already there incarcerated. Cheche was admitted in the hospital right before I had to leave for Puerto Rico. He was too weak to stay home with us, and needed to be hospitalized immediately.

-24-

THE DEATHS OF A FATHER AND A SON

As I mentioned in my previous chapter, I received news about my father's death and quickly made arrangements to fly out to Puerto Rico for Dad's burial. I was already stressed out with all the pressure of having to deal with my brother Cheche's situation, and unfortunately, I couldn't stay behind to continue helping him.

The very next day, I left to Puerto Rico from Newark Airport and arrived in San Juan Airport late that evening. I hadn't notified anyone about my trip, so I asked a cab driver to take me to my destination for only $5. He laughed at me and then thought that I was a crazy nut. Then he declined because his fare was $50, and I was $45 short. Fortunately for me, another gentleman came along, paid his fare, and I convinced the cab driver to allow me to tag along with them and to take the $5 from me as if it was an extra bonus. The other passenger was going through the same exact route that I had to go through. The cab driver finally agreed and took me straight to the funeral home where my dad's wake was being held. I paid him the $5 then he left to take the other passenger to his destination.

As I entered the funeral home, everybody suddenly got quite and turned their attention toward me. They kindly greeted me and gave their condolences as I made my way through to greet everyone. As I approached Dad's coffin, everyone in silence observed to see how or what would I do or how I would react. But the Lord gave me an unbelievable strength and I gracefully kept calm and composed myself as a gentleman and a child of God. There were family members at the wake that I didn't see since I had left Puerto Rico when I was eleven years of age. I admit that my father's family were all very loving with me and asked me not to worry about anything, that they were taking care of all the expenses. I was grateful to them for that and thanked them.

The next day, we all met at the cemetery for the burial ceremony. A week before my father died, I had written him a letter about the plan of salvation in Christ the Lord. I handed the letter to his youngest sister who had been still living in north Newark. She recently had booked flights to visit the family in Puerto Rico and to see how Dad was doing. She was always concerned about Dad after his separation from Mom. Well, after giving her the letter, I asked that she immediately give him the letter upon her arrival.

Unfortunately, Dad died before she can get to Puerto Rico, so she returned the letter to me with the bad news of his death. My heart grieved, fearing the worst, and I thought that Dad lost his soul to the hell fire until the Lord comforted me and reminded me of the time when Dad had given his heart to Jesus. A week later, after my return to the States, the Lord gave me a revelation via a dream regarding Dad's salvation. I won't go into all the details, but I believed God and never doubted him for a moment. God speaks to those that seek him. God loves to comfort and to talk with his people. It is not only for those that lived during Old Testament times, but also for all who seek his will. Without faith, it is impossible to please God (Hebrews 11:6, NIV). Dad had given his heart to Christ in plain public view outside our house on Delavan Avenue. I witnessed this myself, and at the time, I thought to myself that this was ridiculous (I didn't know Jesus back then). When I gave my heart to Christ, I realized the importance of it. It no longer was ridiculous, and it was something that I learned to appreciate as I got closer to the Lord. Both the apostle Paul and Mark mentioned some of these things in the New Testament.

> I am not ashamed of the gospel, because it is the power of God for the salvation of everyone who believes: first for the Jew, then for the Gentile. For in the gospel a righteousness from God is revealed, a righteousness that is by faith from first to last, just as it is written: "The righteous will live by faith."
>
> Romans 1:16–17 (NIV)

> That if you confess with your mouth, "Jesus is Lord," and believe in your heart that God raised him from the dead, you will be saved. For it is with your heart that you believe and are justified, and it is with your mouth that you confess and are saved. As the Scripture says, "Anyone who trusts in him will never be put to shame." For there is no difference between Jew and Gentile-the same Lord is Lord of all and richly blesses all who call on him, for, "Everyone who calls on the name of the Lord will be saved."
>
> Romans 10:9–13 (NIV)

> If anyone is ashamed of me and my words in this adulterous and sinful generation, the Son of Man will be ashamed of him when he comes in his Father's glory with the holy angels.
>
> Mark 8:38 (NIV)

On the night I returned home from Puerto Rico, approximately one week later, the Holy Spirit spoke to my heart while I was still on the plane talking to an artist about music. The Lord's message to me was clear. He made it clear to me that on that very night, he was taking brother Cheche home to be with him forever. That his life had come to an end and was no longer going to be suffering, not ever again. After arriving at Newark Airport, I got into a cab and arrived at Mary's house (it's where I had been staying before heading out to Puerto Rico). I asked Mary about Cheche's well being and asked her to call the hospital immediately for an update. After she called the hospital, the doctors affirmed my brother's death. He died within an hour or less after my arrival. He had finally gone home to be with the Lord. I shared with my family about what the Holy Spirit had shown me on the plane back home. The Lord finally took him home, just as he promised. Jesus prepared my heart and gave me the strength I needed to cope with all that had been happening with our family. We were sad but also happy knowing that he had gone home to be with the Lord in his holy presence. The devil may have killed or destroyed his body, but the Lord saved his soul and spirit for all eternity.

Dad and Cheche died three months after I had surrendered my life to Christ—-within one week of each other, exactly seven days apart. Seven is God's perfect number. Dad died on December 9, at regional hospital in Arecibo Puerto, Rico, and Cheche died on December 16, 1983 at university hospital in Newark (four months short of his thirtieth birthday). Finally, there was no more suffering, no more alcohol, no more drugs, and no more pain. It was finally over for them. Their habits finally caught up with them and took them before their time to their graves. Dad was fifty-eight years old when he died, and Cheche was twenty-nine. Cheche had caught AIDS and Dad's liver gave out on him. What a way to go! The good news was, they both given their hearts to Christ and made it to heaven. I have a logo in mind that says, "Say no to drugs and to alcohol" and say, "Yes to Jesus." Hallelujah!

-25-

KATO'S CONVERSION

I had not seen Kato for some time, until I traveled to Puerto Rico for our father's funeral.

At the news of our father's death, the very next day, I jump on the next plane to Puerto Rico. The very next day after arriving, the ceremonial was to take place, and since Kato was incarcerated, I asked an uncle and police officer (one of Dad's brothers') at the wake, to see if he can pull some strings and have Kato come out to the funeral for Dad's burial. Also, I asked my uncle to talk to the authorities, and see if they would remove his handcuffs for the duration of the ceremonial gathering. My uncle, moved with passion, agreed, and spoke with the proper authorities, and permission was granted for Kato to be united with me and the family, and without the handcuffs, under my uncle's supervision.

The very next day we all drove out to the cemetery and after about five minutes, my uncle and the authorities arrived with Kato and removed his handcuff, immediately, at arrival. As soon as we saw each other, we walked towards one another, embraced, and hugged. As we hugged, I kissed him on his right cheek and told him that both Jesus and I loved him. After the ceremony was over, the authorities drove him back to his prison cell.

Here is where things get really interesting. When my brother Kato arrived at the cemetery for the funeral, immediately I hugged him and told him that the Lord Jesus and I loved him. I was carrying a Bible with me under my arms. I know that when he first saw me with the Bible under my armpit, he must have immediately thought that I was some kind of freaky religious fanatic and a nut. I'm not sure what he thought of it, but he stayed quiet. I knew it was the perfect opportunity to share the gospel with him, so I did. Let me cut to the chase.

Many years later, after we had both been back in the States, we were reminiscing about that very same day in Puerto Rico. He revealed to me that upon returning to his prison cell, the power of the Holy Spirit fell upon him and he immediately received the Holy Spirit and the Lord baptized him with the Holy Ghost; the speaking of tongues (1 Corinthians 12:1–12). He confessed to me that when I hugged him at the cemetery, he felt something so very different in my hug, but could not understand what it was that he was feeling, until after the Lord baptized him in his prison cell. He said that he felt the same presence in his cell that he had felt at the cemetery when I hugged him. It was God's presence. He had not known God's presence prior to this. He said that when the Lord baptized him that very same day, upon his returned to the cell, that not until then, he had not realized that it was God's presence he had been feeling when I hugged him. What an amazing God! I had no clue that the Lord was working his wonders on Kato as I was hugging him. It was Kato's conversion to Christianity. He spoke in a different tongue and God filled him with his Holy Spirit (1 Corinthians 12:4-11).

Kato felt free for the first time in a long time from all his worries and burdens. Although he was incarcerated, he was a free man in his heart. That's the God I serve, Halleluyah. It was after that experience with the Lord that Kato started seeking God.

-26-

LIFE AS A CHRISTIAN

My life as a Christian began in a small little church in Elizabeth, New Jersey where the people were seriously seeking God's holiness. It was here where I committed my life wholeheartedly to the Lord Jesus.

It was a Sunday night on September 4, 1983, when I surrendered my life to the Lord. Fall was quickly approaching, and temperatures were dropping fast. As the church service started, the church choir sang and worshiped God unanimously. They praised the Lord with loud voices and danced and clapped their hands to their King—Jesus. One can easily feel God's presence in the building and his Spirit flowing with power in Jesus Christ name. Before this, I had never been in a church where the people praised God with so much vigor. It was as if heaven came down to earth. Excitement filled everybody's hearts with joy and love, and they could not help but rejoice and shout for the Lord. I was in complete awe of everything that was going on around me; I was flabbergasted. The music went on for about an hour or so. Afterward, the preacher called for testimonies, and people spoke about miracles they've received during the week. To my amazement, everyone that spoke and testified had something positive to say. Prior to this, I've never heard of such things. The preacher then proceeded forward with the preaching of the gospels—one of the four gospels in the New Testament. My heart was totally captivated, and I was at awe from the very start of the service. At the end of the preaching and as I struggled to walk to the front of the church near the altar, I finally surrendered my heart to Jesus, and Christ became my Lord and savior. Suddenly, I found myself weeping like a baby, and I couldn't stop crying for nothing in the world. I didn't understand what was happening to me until sometime later as I had been seeking the Lord fervently. He made me understand that he had cleansed me with his blood, and I no longer was a sinner but a righteous person in his presence (2 Corinthians 5:21 and Romans 10:4). The Holy Spirit touched my heart and changed my life forever. It was an amazing experience that I shall never forget in my life. Gradually, the Lord started showing me his new way of life and what it meant to serve Christ. I felt God's love permeating through my spirit, soul, and body; and he renewed my mind with his word, and he became the main source of my living.

I had never lived a Christian life like this before. As I mentioned in earlier chapters, I didn't know there was a difference between the religion I grew up in and this one. I was now experiencing many wonderful beautiful things in the Lord because I had given my heart to Christ and finally understood God's calling for my life. The Lord filled my heart with his spirit and with his eternal love. This was something I never had before. In fact, I always thought that I was a Christian until the day I gave my heart to Christ and became a born-again Christian like it is written in the Holy Bible. For the first time, I realized an enormous difference between both religions. From the moment I gave my heart to Christ, all I wanted to do was tell everyone about him. I wanted to share the gospel day and night. I was on fire for Christ and the devil hated it. I was never the same after that. Christ gave me a new heart and a new mind to follow him. He became the center of my life, and from that day forward, I lived my life for God. All I wanted to do after that was to please the Lord in everything.

God finally got all my attention, and to tell you the truth, I loved every minute of it; it was all worth it.

Satan no longer governed my life, and I no longer belong to him. His days with me are over, and I have had enough of his atrocities against me and my family. Jesus was now my new Lord, and nothing the devil would do would ever get me to retreat. With the help of the Lord, God helped me prevail over the evil one, and Christ gave me victory over my enemy, the devil. The old me was gone for good, and the new me in Christ was here to stay. What an amazing God I serve. He is an awesome God, and he is great! He took away all my sins, my pains, my hurts, my afflictions and nailed them all on the cross via Jesus. I'm grateful to God for all he's ever done for me and for endowing me with his precious love. Truly, he's a loving God (John 3:16).

That night that I accepted Jesus Christ in my heart, the pastor prayed for me, and the burdens were lifted from my shoulders. I was a free man in Christ. Free from all sin and delivered in righteousness to serve the Lord God—hallelujah! Satan's strongholds and the chains of darkness that had me bound were finally broken, and I was free to go serve the Lord. Satan no longer owned me, and I became a man of God and a man of faith for the kingdom of God. The glory is of the Lord. What an amazing experience. I shall always cherish these wonderful moments and forever be grateful to God and thankful to the Lord Jesus; he is my King.

I've become a warrior for Christ and the presence of the Lord has been with me wherever I go. I rejoiced in my God and the blood of Jesus has cleansed me and washed me from all my sins (1 John 1:7). Luke writes in the New Testament, "In the same way, I tell you, there is rejoicing in the presence of the angels of God over one sinner who repents" (Luke 15:10, NIV).

-27-

THE WORSHIP TEAM

During the first three months of my conversion to Christianity, I lost both my father and my brother Cheche to alcohol and drugs. It was devastating to lose two members of the same family within a week of each other. But the Lord sustained me, favored me, and graced me with his presence; his strength was sufficient for me. A year later, after being a regular member in the church, I joined the outreach worship team, "Alma y Espiritu" (Soul and Spirit) and played guitar with this worship team. On Thursdays and Saturdays, we went out to the streets, played music, and preached God's word fervently, winning many souls for Christ in Jesus's name. God's glory was being manifested, and we were favored with his grace. After about another year, the Lord himself asked me to join the church's main worship team via revelation—a dream. The Lord's dream to me was confirmed when the pastor asked me to prepare myself to play with the church's main worship team. I started out playing percussion (congas), and eight months later, I switched over to playing the guitar with them and worshiped the Lord.

Things were moving along gracefully, and my life as a Christian was changing rapidly as I embraced my new faith. Every day was a new beginning for me, and as a born-again Christian, I began seeing things God's way. I quickly understood God's truth and accepted his will for my life. It was the best thing that had ever happened to me. I didn't know how good it was to serve the Lord until I started playing my instrument for him. The benefits that came with it overjoyed me. Every day I was learning something new about God, and it all fascinated me. Now that I had given my life to God, I could no longer live a day without Christ. He fulfilled all my needs and saturated me with his love. Had I known that serving God was so good, I would have given my heart to Christ years earlier.

I am extremely appreciative of God for his love and for grafting me into his kingdom and service. His timing is perfect. As I continued seeking God and attended weekly fellowships, my life moved forward in a positive way, and as I've mentioned throughout the book. I learned to be submissive to God's will and to his calling; I've willingly succumbed to his will. The more I read and studied his word, the more it's captivated me and overwhelmed me with his love. I've learned that with Jesus, I have everything I've ever needed, and he provides all my needs (Philippians 4:19).

As I got closer to God, my life continued to prosper with Barbie alongside of me. God started blessing us and using us for his glory.

MEETING BARBIE

Barbie and I attended the same church in Elizabeth. It was the same church where I had been converted, and we were each involved in the same adult youth group, though I was also involved with the Outreach Musical Worship Team. Occasionally, I said my hello's to her or interacted with her, and with the others during our Thursdays' fellowship group. During one Saturday night church service, I happened to look her way where she was sitting, and it so happened that when I looked, she also looked my way unanimously, and things gradually took off from there.

After she glanced my way, I noticed how pretty she was with her big brown eyes. At the beginning, I had not thought much of it, but afterward, as we both started getting to know one another, it was obvious that the Lord had staged our acquaintances. Before anyone knew it, we gotten engaged, and eight months later, we got married in church, and God blessed our union. We got married October 12, 1985; two years after my conversion, and the grace of the Lord was with us..

During this time Kato was released from Puerto Rico's prison (before Barbie and I were married), he returned to New Jersey, but shortly after his arrival, he was apprehended again for skipping his parole for crimes he had committed in New Jersey, before leaving for Puerto Rico. He was incarcerated at Marlboro, New Jersey State Prison. Kato was still seeking God from his conversion in Puerto Rico when he was apprehended in New Jersey. One of my uncles and I always went to visit him. We ministered the gospel to Kato and took him personal items, as he needed them. Our visit always made him feel good, and he greatly appreciated them. Sometime later, after Kato's release from prison, he followed and sought after the Lord and committed his life to Christ.

LULU IN PRISON

By this time the law had caught up with Lulu, and she too was incarcerated for crimes she had committed with Cheche before he was placed behind bars. She was held at the woman's penitentiary prison in Clinton, New Jersey, and sentenced for five years. Our brother Cheche had served his five-year term and was released while Lulu was incarcerated, but by the time Lulu would be released, Dad, Cheche and Kato were all in their graves.. Lulu had surrendered her life to Christ while being incarcerated. Barbie and I went to see her periodically and helped strengthen her in the Lord. We ministered God's love to her as the Spirit of the Lord guided us.

It was always hard leaving her behind when visiting hours were over, but unfortunately, there's a price to pay for the crimes we commit (Romans 13:1–5). Although God had forgiven her, man and the judicial law did not; she was prosecuted for her crimes by man's law. The law never likes to forgive. Nevertheless, every time we had gone out to the prison, we encouraged her to continue seeking God's presence. It gave her much hope, faith, and mostly the love of God she needed in Christ the Lord to endure her remaining time behind bars.

Anne and mother both sought the Lord after my conversion to Christianity. Gradually, the Lord was grafting into his kingdom all my family members one by one.

Lulu continued to go to church services after her released from prison, but then the problems and burdens of the world pulled her away, and she felled victim to the devil's evil schemes. Despite her backsliding, she still loved God, and God was still watching over her.

MARY BACKSLIDES

Meanwhile, Mary and her husband backslid and were back to their former ways. They moved around a lot, up and down the east coast, and as time went by and things continued to worsen, they separated and divorce a few years down the road. By this time, Mary was left to fend for herself, but now she was back on drugs, abandoned and back to the streets on her own. She was addicted to drugs again and did whatever she had to do to survive her addiction. Day and night she was hanging out in the streets trying to get for herself her daily fix. Every day was the same thing for her. It was a very hard life she endured due to her drug addiction. She no longer had a marriage and was free to do as she wished and men took advantage of her condition. She suffered much at the hands of men who thought she was worth nothing and used her as if she was a no-body. She was paying a hard price for her way of life. It was a life without hope and without any love.

When a person is a junkie, they're lucky if even their own family members have compassion on them. That's just the way it is. Sometimes, family members are the first to turn their backs on them. The only friends they have are those in their circles who are hooked to the same lifestyle. Many just don't want to be bothered with them, and they forget that these people are also human beings who are hurting and desperately need our help. What would Jesus do? Would he turn his back on a junkie, or would he stretch out his hand and extend his love toward that person? God loves all humans alike and he sent his Son to die for all humanity. What we need to do first is to start by praying for them and then ask God to show us how or what can we do to help them out. The Lord Jesus clearly stated in his word that he came for those who were sick and not for those who were well off.

> While Jesus was having dinner at Levi's house, many tax collectors and "sinners" were eating with him and his disciples, for there were many who followed him. When the teachers of the law who were Pharisees saw him eating with the "sinners" and tax collectors, they asked his disciples: "Why does he eat with tax collectors and 'sinners'?" On hearing this, Jesus said to them, "It is not the healthy who need a doctor, but the sick. I have not come to call the righteous, but sinners."
>
> Mark 2:15–17 (NIV)

In other words, Jesus died for sinners in need of a savior. Just like my family and I were in need of a savior, you too are in need of Jesus. He is the only way to inherit eternal life.

Maybe you are not one of these people who used drugs or ever committed any crimes before. But the fact that you are a born sinner and there are no exemptions, it makes you an outcast from the presence of the Lord, and God will judge you for your crimes (sins).

-28-

KATO BACKSLIDES

At this point, Kato was doing really good, and he was going to church regularly on weekends and following after the Lord. God had touched his heart, and he was doing his best to please the Lord. He cleaned up his act and gotten himself a good job and a vehicle to get back and forth to work. Also, he was a handyman and liked fixing things around the house. I hadn't seen him this peaceful and calm in a long time. Kato was finally doing things appropriately for the glory of God, and he was feeling really happy. He was staying away from the streets and had stopped doing drugs and all the crazy stuff he had been doing for a long time. He was a new man in Christ, and the Lord was with him.

He liked playing the guitar and loved singing songs for the Lord. He had a great voice for singing. Singing was something I always lacked; I couldn't sing for nothing in the world, but he was really good at it. He looked a lot like Dad, sang and played the guitar like Dad, and even had many of Dad's gestures. He was a very handsome young man and attracted women everywhere—something my brothers and I all had in common. During this time, he stayed away from his previous neighborhoods and kept out of trouble and served the Lord.

As time went by, things sort of started changing with Kato and I noticed something just wasn't right. Something was distracting him from God, which caused me to get concerned for him. I knew him well, and I knew when things were wrong with him. God had given me wisdom and discernment to know when the enemy was interfering, so I immediately got into prayer and asked God to show me what was going on with my brother. Kato knew that I can see right through him when things were wrong no matter what it was. I like to call these kinds of situations spiritual insight and/or God sightings. Whatever was going on with him had definitely affected his walk with the Lord. After a few attempts, I finally got him to talk about it and he shared his concerns with me. I tried encouraging him to put it all behind him, but he was hurt and the only comfort he found was drugs. I guess he didn't give God enough time to heal his broken heart.

He retreated to roaming the streets of Newark and went back to hanging out at Dayton Street projects with his friends from the past.

This was bad news because just about all his friends from the past were doing drugs, and it meant that he was back to his old ways. Kato was still sort of a new Christian and wasn't yet mature enough in the Lord to handle such blows. The enemy knew this well and took advantage of it. Satan new Kato loved God and that he was trying to please him as best as he could. The devil knew that Kato's foundation in the Lord wasn't yet solid enough to fight him back with power and authority.

Unfortunately, drugs got the best of Kato, and Satan once again shifted his claws into my brother's life as in the past. By this time, Kato was far too gone and had no strength left in him to call upon the Lord for help. I'm sure he prayed whenever he could, but he was way too weak spiritually to fight back and didn't have the will power to walk away from drugs. Jesus was the only one able to deliver him, but the addiction on drugs gave him no room to call on Jesus. That's just the way it is when we turned back to our old ways. In the gospel of Matthew, Jesus said, "That when a man returns to his old ways, that his situation would be much worse than the first time." Friends, that's exactly what happened to my brother Kato, and it can happen to anyone of us if we weaken our faith in Christ (Matthew 12:43-45).

Kato had returned fully to the streets. He had a son and a daughter whom he cared for a lot, but his drug addiction got in the way of everything. Today I pray that his children understand that the only reason their father wasn't around was because of his drug addiction and because he didn't want them to see him that way. He may not have been the perfect father or the greatest dad to his children, but he loved them. Both his children look a lot like him. His son is his very spit image, except that he's a lot taller and his daughter has his eyes and face with a beautiful smile and dimples.

KATO'S DEATH

Unfortunately, after his backsliding to drugs, he cut his life short and ended up dying from AIDS just like our other brother Cheche. The Lord God had mercy on Kato before he passed on to be with Jesus. I had made it my business to reach out to him via a telephone call to Georgia from New Jersey; he was living in Georgia at the time with Mary. As we spoke on the phone I was sensing his weakness, but I pressed on and encouraged him to reconcile his heart with the Lord. He willingly prayed with me, reconciled with Christ, and afterwards, we prayed for his children. He asked God to watch over them, knowing that he wasn't going to make it. He made me promise that I would always keep them in their prayers, and that's exactly what I do to this very day. He wanted them to know that he really loved them and that he was sorry that he couldn't be there for them. After prayer we said our goodbyes knowing it was the last time we speak. The next day, early morning, he went home to be with the Lord. The Lord had moved my heart to call him the day before, indicating that he was taking him home, and I obeyed him. God's timing is perfect. What an awesome God we serve. The scriptures do tells us that there is a sin unto death; meaning, there are things we do in life that we do wrong, that bring destruction to our health. By these same actions, we bring sickness and death to our bodies; at least that's what I understood it to be, and as long as a person doesn't renounce the Lord, God will forgive them their sins, even on their death bed. I believe that the sin that God doesn't forgive: is when a person rejects Jesus. All other sins God can forgive. My siblings' sins led them to death, but it wasn't for rejecting Jesus, but for abusing their bodies with the use of drugs. Even so, God gave them life when he took them home to be with the Lord. Nevertheless, there are other sins that can easily bring death to us, e.g., killing another person by premeditated murder. This will bring judgment and death to us by those that uphold the law, and that can also be a sin unto death (Romans 13:1–5).

> If anyone sees his brother commit a sin that does not lead to death, he should pray and God will give him life. I refer to those whose sin does not lead to death. There is a sin that leads to death. I am not saying that he should pray about that. All wrongdoing is sin, and there is sin that does not lead to death.
>
> 1 John 5:16–17 (NIV)

The last time I saw Kato alive was one day, when Barbie and I went to visit my mother at her apartment in Seth Boyden, and I remember saying to Barbie, "this is the last time we will see my brother alive." He was already plagued with AIDS. Indeed, it was the very last time we saw him alive. The Holy Spirit had given me this discernment.

It was a bittersweet feeling that my brother Kato had gone from us, but it was also a glorious feeling to know that he actually made it to heaven after all he had been through. Kato died at:

Memorial Medical Center in Savannah, Georgia, on: February 24, 1988; he was thirty; three days short of his thirty-first birthday. My family and I mourned his death, but rejoiced knowing he went to be with the Lord, Jesus.

-29-

LULU'S PRISON RELEASE AND DEATH

There was another big blow yet to come: the passing of my sister Lulu.

Finally, after serving a five year term, Lulu's imprisonment came to a close. She completed her allotted time in prison as required by the judicial courts in New Jersey. The day she was released, my wife Barbie and I waited for her to walk out the prison door, and afterward, we drove her home. It was the happiest day of her life. The Lord commanded his people to visit those in need. Regardless of whom they are and where they've been, our job is to forgive, provide as the Lord leads, and mostly demonstrate our love toward them, with our actions (Matthew 25:37–46).

Prison was no place for such a beautiful lady as she was. She was smart, intelligent, and beautiful. She was an amazing young lady, but the world and Satan had a grip on her, and she got involved with the wrong kind of people. She had been committing crimes and all sorts of atrocities that I would have never ever dream of doing. She dated the wrong kind of men who had no kind of future to look forward to and did nothing but stand on street corners dealing dope all day long. It seemed that she wasn't afraid of anything.

The only thing these men cared about was sex, drugs, and dirty money, which came from the sale of drugs. There were one or two guys that really cared about her, but they still were dealing dope, and all that did for her, was sucked her in deeper. She was living a pure life of darkness. It seemed that every man she dated had the same thing in common; they loved dealing drugs.When the authorities caught up with her, she had told me (while visiting her in prison), that she was serving her time in prison for robbing a bank. Another source told me that it was for a breaking an entry, and that she and Cheche tied up a man and an elderly lady with rope and that the elderly lady had gotten hurt while she was being tied down by my siblings. Whatever the case was, my sister paid the price behind bars.

After her release from the prison, she went to church a few times with me, but not a whole lot. She had gone back to live with a girlfriend of hers in Newark and the distance to church was far for her to travel without a car. Unfortunately, things took a wrong turn for her while she was struggling to survive on her own with her two daughters who had gone to live with her. The pressures of life burdened her and having to keep up with her daughters without resources, wasn't so easy for her. Bills were hard to pay, and as a convict, no one would give her a job. That's when she had to leave her apartment to go live with her friend.

Having to feed yourself and two grown daughters without a job did not come by easy for her. Pressures kept compounding on her, and desperation set in, causing her to fall deeper into a hole. Unfortunately, the system (our government) doesn't make it easy for former inmates to live in society. Instead of helping them with the proper resources, all they do is turn their backs. She loved her two girls and wanted to give them the world, but it was difficult for her. Not being able to work hampered her hopes of having a second chance at life, and both she and her daughters were paying hard for the circumstances they were in. Her girls had grown up without their mom, and this really made things much harder for them because it was the first time in a long time that they had their mom back with them, but the circumstances surrounding them caused them to separate again. As it was, her daughters had been suffering enough living without their mom. So one can only imagine what they all been through. All they wanted was to be able to live together as a family, and that too didn't last too long.

Lulu was finally excited to be with her daughters. I remembered how excited she was when she told me she was finally getting an apartment to live with them. Due to their circumstances, their dreams were shattered, heartbroken, and devastated. This was a big blow for all of them.

It's never easy to try and make up for time loss with your children. A mother can try and do her best to bring love and comfort to her children, but that's never going to be easy. It takes courage and lots of work. All parties involved have to make an effort to cooperate to make things work so that things don't fall apart. Lulu tried the best she could. There were times she called me crying. The pressures were compounding daily, and she was losing her grip. I tried consoling her, but even so, it was hard for her as each day went by.. Due to her circumstances, she couldn't keep her family together. How hard this was on her. She wanted her daughters to have a good future and not live life the way she did. She was devastated, knowing she couldn't do much to help her daughters whom she loved so much and yearned to be with. This broke her heart, and after a meltdown, she returned to drugs.

Sometimes we can't blame children for being bitter and resentful toward their parents, but God heals all wounds. We just need to give the Lord Jesus a chance and try to understand the circumstances. My two nieces suffered a lot, and all I can say is allow Jesus to heal your wounds, and he will heal them. Taking just one day at a time will help a hurting heart recover slowly with the right counseling and by surrounding your lives with positive people who can have a positive influence on you. It doesn't mean that things will be easy, but if one tries to do their part, God will give us the strength we need to overcome all negativity and have victory in his Son's name, Jesus Christ.

Lulu died at university hospital in Newark, on October 12, 1989; four years after my wedding anniversary, at age thirty-three to drugs. She was diagnosed with AIDS. She contracted the deadly disease from sharing the same syringe with Cheche.

The last time I saw my sister Lulu alive and talking was at the university hospital. I had gone with Barbie to see her, and when we got there, we talked a bit, made her laugh, and said funny jokes, but I also knew that it was the very last time I would see her well. The Spirit of the Lord had indicated to have her reconcile with Christ because she wasn't going to speek again, after that day. We prayed for her, she reconciled with Jesus, and asked me to tell her daughters that she loved them with all her heart. She was afraid, and she knew she wasn't going to make it. Like Kato, she too made me promised that I would watch over her daughters, so once in a while, I do check on them via telephone calls. I asked her to stay strong and not to worry about anything, because God had her back, and was watching over her daughters. I didn't tell her what the Lord had shown me not to stir things up. After our good-byes, I told Barbie what the Lord had shown me, and the next day, it was exactly as the Lord had indicated. She was able to move her eyes, but other than that, she couldn't talk or move, and a week later, the Lord took her to his presence. It was heartbreaking, knowing I would never be able to have her around again. I have missed her dearly, but I will see her again in the Lord's presence the day the Lord comes back for me. God has given me the grace and the strength to endure all the tragedies and the lost of my family.

It hasn't been easy, but in Christ, we have victory. The love he's poured upon me and my family, has been overwhelming. None of us deserved God's love and salvation, but in his grace, it has pleased the Lord to have saved, me and my family. I give God all the glory.

I pray and hope that her daughters can forgive their mom for all her mishaps and for all the wrong decisions she made while she was on drugs. Drugs makes people do crazy things. It even makes them make all the wrong decisions. But that's why Jesus died, so if you're a sinner, you can boldly come to him in repentance and ask for forgiveness of your sins, and that's exactly what Lulu did; she asked his forgiveness and he forgave her. No one is exempt and all are welcome; he died for all humanity.

The apostle Paul writes in the New Testament, "Here is a trustworthy saying that deserves full acceptance: Christ Jesus came into the world to save sinners-of whom I am the worst. But for that very reason I was shown mercy so that in me, the worst of sinners, Christ Jesus might display his unlimited patience as an example for those who would believe on him and receive eternal life" (1 Timothy 1:15–16, NIV).

Sometimes we become the judge of others without knowing what's at stake and/or what they have been through. I have learned that it is better to pray and get godly results rather than to talk and get nowhere. God is never in a hurry to judge anyone. If anything, he's always ready to forgive and to join in on our parade and mingle in with us that we may gladly and willingly serve him (Matthew 9:10–13).

> Be merciful, just as your Father is merciful. "Do not judge, and you will not be judged. Do not condemn, and you will not be condemned. Forgive, and you will be forgiven. Give, and it will be given to you. A good measure, pressed down, shaken together and running over, will be poured into your lap. For with the measure you use, it will be measured to you."
>
> Luke 6:36-38 (NIV)

-30-

LOVE AND GRACE

As a Christian man, I continued to seek the Lord, I matured spiritually, and each day I grew stronger in the Lord one day at a time (2 Peter 3:18). It's good to have knowledge and wisdom, but without God's grace in Christ, it's all in vain. Early in my Christian walk, I quickly learned the importance of having God's grace. No matter how much knowledge we have (and we need knowledge), and no matter how much wisdom we have, we still need God's grace to attract lost souls for Christ. Without grace, I fear we may lack the need to love the needy and the lost souls. What am I saying? I'm saying that as Christians, it is our duty to be filled with the Holy Spirit, so we may not lack to demonstrate God's love to others. It all works together, and we can't separate one from the other. This isn't about us, but about learning to appreciate the things that God has done for each and every one of us, so that we can reach out to the needy and extend a helping hand when it is in our power to do so. People need to see that Christ indeed is in our hearts. That's the difference between being religious and having salvation and knowing God. I like to say that if there's grace, then there is God, and if there is God then there is Christ and if there is Christ, then there is love; and that love is the love of God, via his Son, Jesus Christ (1 Corinthians 13:1–13 and 1 John 4:18-19).

The apostle John writes in the New Testament, "A new command I give you: Love one another. As I have loved you, so you must love one another. By this all men will know that you are my disciples, if you love one another" (John 13:34–35, NIV).

From the moment Jesus cursed the fig tree, that made a statement not only to the Jews, but to all mankind. We should learn from Israel's mistakes. His statement meant the dispensation of God's rejection toward Israel. He had had enough of their ways and was disgusted with their false religious deeds and their hypocrisies. Israel bears no fruit, and because of it, God turned away from them and turned to the Gentiles to produce fruits of righteousness for the kingdom of God. Jesus's disciples were all dumbfounded by the Lord's cursing of the fig tree because the tree wasn't in a season of bringing forth its fruits. Yet Jesus cursed it so it would no longer give fruit. How confused his disciples must have been. The Jews were supposedly the Lord's chosen people to bring forth the word of God to all mankind, but they didn't do that. It doesn't mean God has stopped loving them. In fact, he loves them now more than before and has his eye-lids wide opened on all Israel. Let's not think that for a moment, God has forgotten them, because he hasn't. They forever shall be his love and those that come against them (the Jews), will pay dearly with their lives, unless they repent and find redemption in the savior, Jesus Christ. The problem the Jews had back then, was that they were too busy making their own religious rules and dictating God's word however it pleased them. The worse part of it all was that they had God's word and acted as if they didn't know or understand God's will for their lives. They manipulated religion to fit their personal needs. They even thought that no one other than themselves (Jews only) had a right to God's kingdom. They didn't want others branching in with them as if they owned God. As far as they were concerned, God had cast off all other peoples and nations of the earth, except themselves—the Jewish nation of Israel. We all know that at one time, it was true that they were called to be the chosen ones for the Lord and that they were the ones whom God chose to be a priest of people to all nations. But they were stubborn and continuously failed to obey their God over and over again. The Lord got tired of all their ways and turned to the Gentiles in order that his own people may get jealous and maybe repent and find refuge in their God. Israel and the Jews have paid a hard price for rejecting Christ. History tells us that in the year AD 70, Titus the General and his Roman army went into Jerusalem and destroyed the city of Jerusalem, the temple, and everything in it. Many Jews were killed, and many others were dispersed throughout Europe and many parts of the world. It wasn't until 1948 when Israel became a nation again. Let's pray for them because God still loves them and Jerusalem is still the apple of his eye and God prospers all those that want the best for Israel (Psalms 122:6).

You see, they were lacking God's love, and to make things worse, they didn't allow others to get close to God and receive his grace.

Many Jews today have acknowledged the Lord Jesus as their personal Lord and savior, but the majority of them still reject Jesus as their messiah. If you're Jewish and you're reading this book, I implore you to accept Jesus as Lord. He is Yeshua the Messiah and the Christ. Shalom!

> What then? What Israel sought so earnestly it did not obtain, but the elect did. The others were hardened, as it is written: "God gave them a spirit of stupor, eyes so that they could not see and ears so that they could not hear, to this very day." And David says: "May their table become a snare and a trap, a stumbling block and a retribution for them. May their eyes be darkened so they cannot see, and their backs be bent forever."
>
> Romans 11:7–10 (NIV)

> I do not want you to be ignorant of this mystery, brothers, so that you may not be conceited: Israel has experienced a

hardening in part until the full number of the Gentiles has come in. And so all Israel will be saved, as it is written: "The deliverer will come from Zion; he will turn godlessness away from Jacob. And this is my covenant with them when I take away their sins."

Romans 11:25–27 (NIV)

-31-

MARRIAGE AND GOD

Two years into church serving the Lord, I married Barbie, a wonderful, beautiful young lady from the same church. As I mentioned in chapter twenty-seven, Barbie and I married on October 12, 1985 in Elizabeth, New Jersey; it was an early Saturday afternoon. Our parents are from the Caribbean Islands (Puerto Rico and Cuba) and we're both born and raised in the states. My parents gave birth to me in New Jersey, where I was raised, and Barbie's parents gave birth to her in New York, but then, later on they moved to New Jersey in 1975. Barbie was eleven going on twelve, when her parents relocated to Elizabeth. It was in church where Barbie and I first met, and we were involved in different ministries. I had been playing guitar with the worship team and, she was involved with the adult youth group, and at times the groups intermingled for bible studies and street preaching. Playing for the King of kings and the Lord of lords was a humbling experience for me and one of the greatest experiences. I loved and enjoyed playing for Jesus, and it made me feel really good. It was a privilege to play for the Lord my King—"Jesus."

Throughout the years, I played various instruments for the Lord and did my best to play them as best as I could for God's glory. God accepts sacrifices that come from the heart. I never considered myself to be the best musician, but I sure gave him my best. Besides, the Psalmist writes in the Old Testament, "Sing to him a new song; play skillfully, and shout for joy" (Psalms 33:3, NIV). I played wholeheartedly for Jesus with all my strength, my heart, my mind, my soul, and my spirit; I gave him my all. He was worthy of all the praises and more, and still is worthy to be praised. Playing and singing for the King (Jesus) is the best feeling in the world. It is fulfilling. It was the best years of my life.

Barbie attended to all the house needs, worked, watched laundry, cooked and etc. Our lives were extremely busy, but even so, we still made time for each other (home), God and church. Sometimes it was overwhelming, but we have no regrets for serving the Lord. He kept us busy and involved doing his will. Service was on Saturday nights, Sunday mornings, and Sunday nights. The fact that I was part of the worship team, I had to be at all three services. I learned that to serve the Lord is either a yes or no, but no in-between. The church we came from was a very good church, and their services were in Spanish. I admit that at the beginning, I had a really hard time trying to understand the sermons in Spanish, but I stuck it out, and the Lord blessed me in every sense of the word. Barbie was blessed as well with the ministry on Thursdays and loved participating with group activities. Four times I did missionary trips with members from our own church and with members of our daughter church in Providence, Rhode Island. Missionary trips were tremendously challenging, but the joy and the love that came with it was all worth it.

Every summer during the month of July, the church held a camping retreat (which they still do), and there we bonded with one another as we worshiped the Lord. My wife and I went every year for one or two weeks and spent time there with the church and God glorified himself at the camp ground. This was a spiritual retreat, and the objective here was to have some quality time with one another, but mostly with the Lord. The Lord manifested himself in our lives as we continued to fellowship with him and with one another.

Every day we felt the blessings of the Lord, and Barbie has been a great wife to me from the Lord. God knows I having been perfect, though in weakness, God makes me perfect (2 Corinthians 12:9).

Accustomed to visiting my siblings in prisons made it easy for me to visit the jails throughout the New York, New Jersey and Pennsylvania metropolitan area, and I ministered to the many inmates behind bars. I thank Christ for that. He made me see things differently. I understood these were lost souls in need of the same savior that had saved me and my family. My friends (Christian brothers in Christ) and I led them in prayer and together we prayed the sinners' prayer for salvation and many of them willingly gave their hearts to Christ (Matthew 25:34–46). It was a blessing to see how many prisoners came to the Lord and proclaim Jesus as their personal Lord and savior.

I enjoyed the involvement I had with the church in New Jersey and the activities. Barbie always had dinner ready on time, and we always ate together. She knew I was busy and had time for nothing. Her life as a wife alone was a ministry in itself. Looking back at things, I suggest no member should be getting involved in too many church activities all at the same time. The church usually has plenty of members to help out with for different activities (ministries), and no one person should be doing everything. This gesture takes off a ton of loads off their pastor's shoulders, and frees him up for the more important matters. I had my plate full, but that never was a problem for me. But that doesn't mean that is okay, and we need to learn how to balance our time. We all need time with God before getting involved in any ministry, but it's also essential we spend plenty of time with our love ones as well. But don't neglect to spend much time with God. The more time we spent with him, the more blessed the ministry will be. Balancing our lives between home (family), God (church ministries), work, and friends will always be beneficial and not burdened any member of the congregation. What am I saying? I'm saying that church first starts at home, and if we can't minister our own homes first, how in the world will we be able to minister in the house of God? Please don't misunderstand and/or misconstrue what I'm saying. The church is not to be blame for members who neglect their families. Each head of household should know his or her boundaries, but the church should never be an excuse to justify not spending enough time with your love ones. God forbid, but only the members that allowed themselves to run from "to and fro," (as if there's nothing to do at home), are the ones to blame; I'm referring mostly to the married.

Otherwise, we will run into all sorts of problems, and our marriages will be the first thing affected and attacked by the enemy. I am speaking out of my own personal experience. Keeping things in perspective will always keep things in order. Matthew writes in the New Testament, "But seek first his kingdom and his righteousness, and all these things will be given to you as well. (Mathew 6:33, NIV).

-32-

MARY'S STRUGGLES

One summer evening, Barbie and I decided to take a ride to Newark and visit Anne and her family. We were still living in Elizabeth, and it took about forty-five minutes to get to Anne's. Her residence neared the border of the city of Belleville, which was about five or less minutes away.

After about an hour at Anne's place, the doorbell rang, and to our surprise, it was our eldest sister, Mary. Barbie and I had not seen Mary for quite a while prior to this particular day. When Mary walked in and saw us, she was totally flabbergasted, but she smiled and said hello. I guess she was just as surprised as we were. Talking about right timing! God's timing is perfect, and nothing is a coincidence for him. We exchanged conversations, said a few jokes, and laughed, though at the beginning she was a bit reluctant to sit with us and unsure of what to expect from us. She was nervous, but we got her to calm down and assured her that there was nothing to worry about and that we weren't there to judge her. She seemed tired and exhausted and wasn't too sure how to react around us. She knew Barbie and I had been going to church and that we were walking with the Lord, so she was hesitant to even say anything at all, but I immediately broke the ice and sparked up a conversation with her. After a few minutes, she felt comfortable, and we were able to get her to sit next to us on the couch. Once we got her to sit on the couch, I hugged her and told her that I love her and that Jesus loved her as well. Barbie and Anne also said the same to her. Being that she already knew who Jesus was, I tried not to lecture her. It was through her that I came to the Lord. If she had been high that night, I promise you that it went away from her within the first five minutes of her arrival. Every day, she had been loitering around the streets of Newark, day and night just for a quick fix and a temporary feel-good high.

When she first walked in, the Spirit of the Lord immediately spoke to my heart and made it clear to me that he had sent her there, so that I can minister to her. I was obedient, and after a few jokes, I found a way to spark up a conversation about the love of God without lecturing her. After our conversation started and we had a dialog going, the Holy Spirit gave me discernment and showed me that I needed to pray for her left eye because it was really bothering her. I asked her to let me pray for her eye, and immediately she confessed to us that a burning pain on her left eye and eyebrow had been bothering her all day long. She said that she felt an immediate healing after we had prayed for her and rebuked the demon that was tormenting her. Afterward, I gave her a word of encouragement from the Lord, then we hugged again and, I shared with her how much we all missed her and loved her; this made her cry. We gave her our contact information and asked her not to lose having contact with us and to try and stay in touch. The presence of the Lord was mighty and powerful that night as we ministered God's love to Mary. Mary was touched by his presence, and the love of Christ gave her some tranquility and peace that night.

She had been going through a lot and was very hungry, thirsty, sleepy and tired, and needed much rest. God still loved her and just because she had walked away from him to a life of drugs, it didn't mean that he stopped loving her or that his love for her diminished. He wanted her to know that he still had his eye on her and cared for her well being.

The Holy Spirit loves to minister to people like Mary, and he doesn't reject them. He wants them to see Jesus in light of their shortcomings, and it doesn't matter to God what they have done. A life living in darkness always has its implications. Mary suffered much and lived a cruel life in a world where Satan controlled the atmosphere, and all his surroundings were clouded with shadows of death and where demonic forces kept her bound, blinded, and deceived. It's a lifestyle without any hope for a better life. Not many people make it in this kind of a world, where darkness doesn't allow the light of Christ to shine. But with God, he can take us from the streets to the cornerstone (1 Peter 2:6).

We are ambassadors of Christ to bring and share the good news (the gospel) to all mankind—no exemptions (2 Corinthians 5:20, James 5:19-20 and 1 Peter 4:8). We need to demonstrate God's love to them in a loving manner with our actions. Otherwise, our deeds are dead and worth nothing.

Mary had been backsliding for the longest time and was way over her head. There were many other things in my sister Mary's life, which I dare not say. Just know that if you're living a life without Christ, then chances are that you're living a life in darkness. God judges all sins, regardless of the gravity of our sins. We are in debt with God, and we all need his forgiveness and his salvation. By accepting Jesus as our Lord and savior, we can enter his kingdom for all eternity. Anything other than that is nothing but the biggest lie Satan has ever fabricated.

It was during this time that Mary had gotten divorced from her last husband and left the church, as I mentioned in chapter twenty-seven. Unfortunately, this was a very bad marriage for Mary, and she found herself all alone.. I dare not knock her; after all, she's my sibling. I'm not condoning any of the wrong she's ever done, on the contrary, I'm praising her for staying alive and for her courage to find strength in her God, even though, it came much time later.

Behind every book, there's always a story to tell. Mary didn't sleep well for a long time. All the worries of the world burdened her. I know that some of us will never understand what caused Mary to change. Today we may be fine, but tomorrow can be another story. Mary did many things that many of us wouldn't dream of doing. Nevertheless, God had mercy on her and got her far away from everything she ever knew that dragged her life deep down to the pits of hell. He's an awesome God, and his love endures forever. As I reflect on everything that has happened to our family, I can't help but believe that all this mess really started when we were nothing but a family living in darkness out in Paterson, New Jersey. But the great news is that the Lord has delivered us from the streets to the cornerstone, and that cornerstone is Christ Jesus (Ephesians 2:19-22).

Today, I'm proud to say that Mary is drug free, off the streets and living an extremely peaceful life. Occasionally, she does visit a church here and there, but she has reconciled with Christ. She keeps herself busy with work, home and her pet. This beats being in the streets! Praise the Lord!

MINISTERS AND CHRISTIANS

As I have been writing this part of my Mary's personal and previous life, the Holy Spirit has compelled me to write to all Christians and ministers in today's pulpits. Now this doesn't apply to all ministers or Christians, but it sure does apply to many of us.

I responded to the Lord's calling when he called upon me. I grew up in the ghettos of Newark, and I'm very proud of it. If you're wondering if anything good can come out of the ghettos, then my answer to you is yes; I'm living proof. I love the story in the Bible when Jesus says to Philip to follow him like two of his other disciples had been doing from the town of Bethsaida and especially the part when Philip finds Nathanael and tells him that they had found the Messiah from a town named Nazareth. Nathanael was so surprised that the Messiah was from that town. It seemed that it was a place or a town where the people were looked down upon. No doubt the town was filled with the good, the bad and the ugly; criminals were no exemption. But we really need to be more careful how we look at people and how we treat them. God loves all peoples of the world regardless of the creed, ethnicity, religion, background and social status they come from. That includes all criminals. Jesus died for all, and indeed he is our cornerstone, therefore, take care that you don't stumble (John 1:43-46 and 1 Peter 2:7-8).

-33-

MICHAEL'S MIRACLE

Late on a Saturday night as Barbie and I were crossing the street from our vehicle, we ran into an old acquaintance. We were coming home from church, and it was a bit late when suddenly, we run into Mike Perez. Barbie and I were living right on Elizabeth Avenue in Elizabeth, on the second floor of a hardware store building. Before that night, Michael and I hadn't seen each other for about fifteen years since my parents moved us out of Dayton Street projects. By this time, Barbie and I had been married for about three years. Mike was double parked right in front of my apartment with the trunk of his car opened. We immediately hugged each other and conversed for only a few minutes because he was on his way to perform down the block from me. Barbie was tired so she immediately went upstairs to the apartment after I introduced her to Mike. To find Mike parked in front of my apartment was no coincidence. He didn't know I lived there, and when I saw him, I knew immediately that it was God who placed him there precisely so that I can talk to him about Jesus. My heart was filled with joy and gladness when I saw him; I was flabbergasted. Prior to this incident, I remembered speaking to Mike only one time after a mutual friend gave me his telephone number, and I called him. He was still living in the projects and was surprised to hear from me. He told me that he was also married and was taking one day at a time. When I called Mike, it was quite a few years since I moved out of the community, so you can imagine how overwhelmed we both were to have run into each other. Other than that, I had not seen or heard from Mike. I always wondered if Mike was okay and what he was up too. Whenever the Lord would bring him to my thoughts, I prayed for him and asked God to save him and have mercy on him. I knew the kind of life Mike had been living and I concerned for him. It was definitely a blessing from the sky to run into Mike that night. Mike and I grew up in the projects, and one of his older brothers and I were classmates in grammar school. His brother and I practiced playing guitar together at their parents' apartment in building 4 of the projects. Mike was younger than us, so he and I didn't really hang out together, but we saw of each other quite a bit being that I was around his brother a lot. Whenever I go visit them to practice music with his brother, Mike was usually there practicing his keyboard. Mike has always loved music, and he dedicated lots of his time to it while growing up in the ghettos, as I did. I confessed to you that today, Mike is one of the best key musicians in the city of Newark and in the metropolitan area. He self-taught himself while learning what he could from others. No one knew that Mike was going to be such a great musician, and everywhere he went to play, the people enjoyed watching and hearing him do his thing. Mike is now well-known throughout the entire northeast metropolitan area for his music. He's playing successfully on a professional level with a wonderful group of guys.

Mike's family and mine go way back before Dayton Street projects. One of Mike's aunts was married to one of my uncles (a sibling of my mother's). Mike comes from a family who lived in many ways the same way my family and I lived. His parents faced many of the similar problems, especially with some of their own children. Two of Mike's uncles were best friends with my two older brothers: Cheche and Kato. But let me cut to the chase with Cousin Mike's story.

Mike noticed I was carrying my guitar with me, so he asked me, "Where are you coming from, bro, were you performing somewhere?"

I immediately responded and said, "Yeah, Mike! My wife and I had just got home from church, and I've been playing guitar for God for a few years now."

He was surprised but was very happy for me and said, "Oh, that's cool, bro, nice, man, and that's all right, bro. I'm getting ready myself to go play at the bar right down the block from you."

Then I said, "That's cool, bro, nice. How long have you been performing?"

We spoke for another few minutes before he had to leave for his gig, but I knew I had little time to talk to him about God, so I immediately sparked up a conversation with him about God and pressed upon him that God wanted to save his soul and that God had a plan for him. I continued to tell him about the love of Jesus and that Jesus was able to change his life around just like he had done with me.

Mike knew the kind of life I had with my family, and he can see I was speaking truth to him. I was a living testimony to Mike. I didn't need to make up any stories or come up with a fake act. Mike himself comes from a family of prayer, and his family loves God dearly. Mike was quite taken by me, but because he had to go perform, he couldn't stay to continue our conversation. We said our good-byes and went our separate ways. I went home, and he went to perform at the bar, but while he was performing at the bar, my wife and I were praying for Mike that night at home, after he left us. God had brought Mike to me and wanted me to pray for him because he loved him so much, and he didn't want Mike to lose his soul. God knew I was a man of prayer and knew he can count on me to pray for Mike. After that night, I never saw Mike again because we both had our separate lives and were very busy doing our own thing. He had his life with his music, and I had my life with my music in the Lord. Mike also was married to a wonderful wife from Dayton.

Many years later, after my wife and I moved across country to the state of Texas, I got a surprise telephone call from a nephew of mine who said that he had met Mike Perez and that Mike was there with him and was wanting to speak with me. I immediately said, "Yes, of course, put him on the phone." I was completely blown away—flabbergasted. It was about another fifteen to twenty years since I seen or spoken to Mike after the night on Elizabeth Avenue. God works in mysterious ways. We spoke for about twenty to thirty minutes on the phone, and during the conversation, I was in complete awe of what I was hearing. Mike was telling me about how he had changed his life around and that he no longer was addicted to drugs and had given his life to Christ. He continued and said his marriage was going strong and that he was playing music steady with a salsa band and that they had recently launched their very first CD. I was so happy to hear such great news from Mike. What struck me the most about his conversation was what he had been telling me about himself and the positive changes that were occurring in his life. He said, "Willie, after that night that you spoke to me about the Lord Jesus, my whole life changed around, bro. I got my act together and started doing things right. I had spent five years in prison and that really got to me, bro. I couldn't be with my wife and children whom I love so much, and many times as I sat in my prison cell, I kept thinking about the times you stopped to talked to me about Jesus. The words you spoke to me regarding Jesus made a difference in my life, and I've never been the same. I came out of prison, and ever since I did, I've been clean now for about nineteen years, I don't mess around with drugs anymore and I don't even drink alcohol." I was so taken by his words, and all I could do was thank God for Mike and for hearing my prayers and the prayers of his parents. What an awesome God we serve.

Today, Mike and I stay in touch with each other all the time. Mike and I are like brothers today just like my brothers were with his uncles, and we make sure that everything is okay.

After saying our good-byes on the phone, I praised my Lord Jesus and thanked God for all he had done with Cousin Mike and for all he's still doing with him. Truly, Michael is a miracle from God. Mike had been through a lot growing up with his family and with some of his friends. Drugs had taken a toll on his marriage, and things had gone downhill for him. But now all that changed, and Mike is a different person today. Everybody who knows Mike is so proud of him, especially his parents and his family and me. Mike is a perfect example of what God does when we unite in prayer for the loss. God loves when we pray instead of wasting our time talking bad about others. God never gave up on Mike. The glory is all God's, hallelujah! Praise God!

Why am I bringing up his story? Mike is also a product of what God does when we take time out to talk to people about Jesus. His parents had been concerned for him and had been praying for him for a long time now, but God still hadn't gotten Mike's attention. God was answering their prayers, but they had not seen the results of their prayers yet. God was also looking for someone other than his own family to reach out to him and share with him the gospel. I knew Mike had to go and play, and without getting religious on him, I made the effort to tell him about Jesus and how much the Lord loved him.

Mike is grateful to God and has thanked me for all the times I stopped him in the streets and talked to him about Jesus. With Christian parents that Mike has, God has kept his promised to them about their son. He promised them via his word that Mike would one day be saved (Acts 16:31). Today, Mike is a new man and has been set free from drugs and from a life of destruction. He's happily married with children and grandchildren (2 Corinthians 5:17).

Mike sent me a copy of his CD with a letter attached to it saying how the Lord gave him a second chance. Folks, this is the kind of God we serve. He gives us second chances and more. All we need to do is believe God and allow him to help us. I like to acknowledge his lovely wife as well. Mike put her through a lot because of the problem he had with drugs, but she's a strong woman, and she never gave up on Mike. Through thick and thin, she was there for him. She loved him and kept the faith, never diminishing, not one bit. She fought for her marriage and prevailed. Women need to take her example, and instead of feeling sorry for themselves, they need to call upon God and declare victory over their marriages and their families and not allow the devil to take away from them what God gave them: their man and their children. May God bless her always for being strong for Mike and their lovely children. Indeed she's been the anchor of the family, keeping them close and knit together as a family should be.Today, she is happily reaping the fruits of a happy marriage and a happy family. She helps Mike by working and enjoys life with her family (Proverbs 31:25–31).

Mike is one of many stories I can write about, but I believe that by now, you got the message. With God, all things are possible.

I have allowed the Holy Spirit to evangelize the Gospel of Christ through me and by his grace, we are saved. Today I continue my quest of winning souls for Christ.The glory is for the Lord. Mike's letter to me follows on the next page.

2009

Hey Willie,

God bless. Hope all is well with you and the family. I remembered the last time I saw you, I was so strung out on drugs and the Lord gave me a second chance and I have not looked back. Been cleaned for 19 years and moving on up. Here's the CD I said, "I'd send you." Enjoy it my brother and may the Lord bless you always and your family too.

Stay in touch!

Mike Perez

-34-

ANNE AND MOM MOVED TO RHODE ISLAND

Years later, after I've been serving the Lord and married, my sister Anne and her husband moved their family out of Newark and went north to Rhode Island.

Anne as well as our mother went to the same church that Barbie and I were going to for a good number of years before they left for Rhode Island. Anne lived in Newark all her life, but things in Newark had really been changing rapidly, and gangs had been forming throughout the city and moving into many neighborhoods. Once they found an apartment in Rhode Island, they packed their belongings and left. Prior to their move, I had been going back and forth to Rhode Island because our church had a daughter church there, and as a musician, I was with the worship team visiting the church there quite often. Due to that, Anne immediately had a church to go to, and shortly after that, she had joined their worship team as part of their choir, and she was free to worship the Lord. Rhode Island was a great move for them, and things went well for them.

At the time, our mother was still living in Newark, but I intervened and convinced her to leave Newark and go north to Rhode Island to be near Anne. Mom first declined moving to

Rhode Island, but because she was living in Seth Boyden projects and things were getting out of control there, I was feeling uneasy about her staying there, so one night, I showed up with a truck and a group of my friends without giving her notice, and we moved her right out of Seth Boyden that very night. We drove four hours to Rhode Island to her very own apartment. Had my mom stayed in Seth Boyden projects, I don't think she would have survived on her own living there.

Sometime later, my oldest niece, Fin-Fui moved to Rhode Island as well. There were other relatives living out there, but I wasn't that close to them at the time. I still kept in contact with those relatives, but it was only like whenever I ran into them which wasn't much.

Barbie and I went often to Rhode Island to see Mom and Anne, and sometimes whenever time allowed it, we stop by Fin-Fui's place and other relatives.

Anne later on had to leave the choir at the church due to her health. Her health had gotten frail so she could no longer sing with the worship team. Anne is in God's hands. She goes to church when possible, but when she hurts too much, then she stays home. Anne still loves the Lord as always. Therefore, I say to you, my darling little sister, Anne, hold on to the Lord just a little longer and keep up the faith, for our Lord is with you and he will never abandon you. He knows your pain and your sorrows, and his love for you has not diminished not one bit. Therefore, take hold of his word and find comfort in his love. His coming is very near, sooner than any one of us can ever imagine. Also, Anne had forgiven Dad many years ago after understanding the love of God. The emotional scars she had been carrying are all gone. If by chance some are still lurking around, I trust God will help her through and set her free from them. The Holy Spirit is our helper and will strengthen Anne if need so. Healing doesn't always come easy or happens overnight. It's a process that takes one day at a time. As we heal, God helps us.

One day soon, we shall be with Jesus in his glory and all the pains, hurts, and tears shall all disappear and cease from all our lives. If for some reason our deaths come first, well, not to worry. In the rapture of the church, God will raise the dead in Christ first (1 Thessalonians 4:16). Know this, my darling sister, the psalmist in the Old Testament writes, "Precious in the sight of the Lord is the death of his saints" (Psalms 116:15, niv). That is a promise from our Creator so there's no need to fear. Therefore, little sister, my prayers are with you and your family. Keep the faith and always remember that God loves you and your family. To my darling sister Mary, I say the same. Be blessed, my dear sisters, and know that I love you both dearly.

-35-

OUR PRECIOUS MOTHER "CHEFA"

Many people have always known my mother by the name of "Chefa." As I've written throughout the chapters, my mother didn't have it easy with the problems she faced at home with my older siblings and my father. To put the icing on the cake, as one thing piled upon another, my parents' marriage came to an end.

Now we shall focus about her life while she was living in Rhode Island near my sister Anne.

Our mom loved knitting and sewing, and when we were children, she sewed for us our own clothing in order to help Dad save money. She also loved to crochet and was very good at it. Till today, I haven't met anyone who crocheted like she did. It was something she loved doing, and enjoyed it very much; that was her expertise. At age eighty-three, Mom could no longer crochet; her hands hurt due to osteoporosis and her problem with dementia/Alzheimer. Prior to all these situations in her life, Mom had suffered very much not just with my dad but with others as well. She was outgoing, bright and smart, and loved cooking for the family. She worked when she could and loved to dress pretty. But now that she has Alzheimer's, everything has totally changed for her. She's no longer the mother I once knew. The disease has taken over her life, and she's limited at everything she does. As I write her story, I like to express that there's no love like the love of a mother, with one exception—God. God is the only one besides our mothers whom we can compare them too. Other than that, there is no other comparison.

My mom Chefa is now eighty-five years old and lived with me and my wife Barbie in Texas for about one and a half years, before admitting her into a nursing home due to the disease. The nursing home is about twenty-five minutes away from our home and I visit her periodically. She no longer remembers any of the past and therefore, doesn't suffer about all the things that ever happened with the family and with others. In a way, as much as I hate to admit it, the Alzheimer's has served her as a blessing, and not that I desire for her or anyone else to have this horrible disease, but the fact that she can't remember her past has allowed her to live a peaceful life in her old age. Despite all she's been through, she finally has peace.

As each day goes by, I love her more and more, and I'm aware that at any moment, God can call her home to be with him. Let me change gears now and shift to the point of her story.

Mom was already changing before Barbie, and I moved across country to the State of Texas, but no one really noticed. Due to my disability, I had no longer visit Mom and Anne as much as I used to. But after Barbie and I moved to Texas, I would book a flight whenever it was feasible. By this time, Barbie and I were living in Texas about four years, when suddenly, one day, out of the sky blue, I hear the voice of God.

The voice of God spoke to me audibly, and he said, "Your mother is depressed." I was asleep on my couch when I heard his voice. I immediately got up from my sleep, sat on my couch, and responded by saying, "Depressed, Lord? What do you mean she's depressed?" He didn't say anything else. Barbie was at her job, and it was around late morning when the Lord revealed these words to me. After hearing his voice, I knew God wanted me to do something about my mother's situation. His voice was soft and gentle but was very direct. After hearing his voice, there was no way I was going back to sleep. I immediately prayed and concerned myself with my mother's situation, and after a few minutes, got on the phone and dialed Anne's number in Rhode Island. I shared with Anne what the Holy Spirit had just finished revealing to me, and as we conversed about Mom, Anne informed me that Mom was drinking alcohol every day and that she was out of control. That is what God meant when he told me, that my mother was depressed.

You see, when God speaks, we have to listen carefully and interpret what he is trying to tell us. Had God not spoken to me when he did, I would have probably never known about Mom's condition, and it would have probably been too late to help her. God sees everything, and he was bothered by the fact that my mother was destroying her life, and nothing was being done about it. He knew that I was the only hope she had left for any survival. He did not want Mom to die as a drunkard. I needed to take quick action, so I immediately booked my flight to Rhode Island to get to the bottom of the problem and see if there was anything I can do to help. She too had backslid from the Lord's will for her life. Mom was too weak physically and spiritually to fight it off on her own. She became a danger to herself. Indeed, this was a spiritual battle (Ephesians 6:12).

God was depending on me 100 percent to find a solution for my mother and resolve the problem as soon as possible before it would be too late.

I was flabbergasted and couldn't believe my mother's situation. After so many years that she had been set free from drinking alcohol, she was now addicted again, and this time around, it was a lot worse. This was the very cause of my father's death. I was upset with her situation, because it was one of the main factors that cause my parents' divorce, and now she was doing the same exact thing, but worse. This news broke my heart into little pieces, and all I could think of was how can she do such a thing knowing very well that it was the source of so many problems at home with Dad and his death? For sure, I thought she wasn't going to survive much longer than a few months. I was crushed.

After arriving in Rhode Island and stepping in her apartment, as I assessed the situation, it was worse than I could ever imagine. I tried talking to her and advised her carefully what would happen if she continued drinking. But it was to no avail. While I was there, I found a rehabilitation center for her with room and board where she would be detoxicated, but she declined. I couldn't force her to go, therefore, my hands were tied. I was with her one week before returning home and even offered for her to come home with me to Texas, but she also declined.

Mom was consuming a bottle or more of wine per day. The second day I was there, I found her completely drunk and knocked out on her bed with the door to her apartment opened and a pot of rice cooking on the stove. Had I not gone to Rhode Island and listened to the voice of the Lord God, I promise you that my poor mother would have been burned alive drunk, and incinerated..

My mother's alcohol problem mentally impaired her ability to make capable decisions. She needed supervision day and night and could no longer live on her own. I did whatever I could during the week I spent there with her and because she refused and declined professional help, I didn't have much of a choice but to return home without her. On my way back home, I was the most miserable person in the world. I thought I failed the Lord. But God wasn't done with Mom yet, and I had not failed him. God was preparing everything for Mom's arrival to Texas on a different occasion.

One can only imagine what went through my mind. I was devastated. What a curse this was.

I knew I had to control my emotions and stand firm because she was still my mother. But the pain she caused me during the week I was there was extremely hurtful. Once I got back home, I knew there was only one person I can count on who wouldn't let me down, and that was God. I pleaded with him almost every day to keep watch over Mom and not to allow her to die a horrible death. I reminded him of his promises. Finally, after another two years, (and I will spared you the details), the Lord opened a door for Mom to successfully come out to Texas, and live with me and Barbie.

It was the happiest day of my life to see my mother again alive and well. Well, she wasn't actually well, but she had life and that's all that matter. My mother weighed about eighty-four pounds, and as the months went by, she gradually gained weight. Before admitting her to the nursing home a year and a half later, my mother was up to 139 pounds. She had gained all her weight and exceeded it. What an awesome God we serve. Halleluyah, God is great!

She's never again had the need to drink any liquor, and because of the disease she has, she doesn't even remember any of it. For that, I praise the Almighty God. It was God who made everything possible because of what Jesus had done for us; he died on the cross. May God be praised and to him be the glory.

My mother reconciled with her Lord as soon as she stepped foot in Texas. It's true that now she lives in a nursing home, but the day she dies (unless the rapture of the church takes place first), God will call her home to be with him for all eternity. Satan tried very hard to take her soul, but God prevailed.

> The acts of the sinful nature are obvious: sexual immorality, impurity and debauchery; idolatry and witchcraft; hatred, discord, jealousy, fits of rage, selfish ambition, dissensions, factions and envy; drunkenness, orgies, and the like. I warn you, as I did before, that those who live like this will not inherit the kingdom of God.
>
> Galatians 5:19–21 (NIV)

With God's help, Satan lost the battle against my mother, and in Christ Jesus, we are victorious. Prayer is the key element to keeping the faith (Matthew 7:7-8). It is of most important to the church of Christ. God gives us the victory, and that's exactly what he did for my mother and my family.

The Lord commands us to take care of our parents (Exodus 20:12). The apostle James writes in the New Testament, "Religion that God our Father accepts as pure and faultless is this: to look after orphans and widows in their distress and to keep oneself from being polluted by the world" (James 1:27, NIV).

God is great, hallelujah!

-36-

AS FOR ME AND MY HOUSE, WE SHALL SERVE THE LORD

Barbie and I have continued to devote our lives to God in Texas where we now live, and we congregate weekly for worship in a small congregation near home. Throughout the years, we have had our mishaps like any other marriage, but we are still growing strong and moving forward with our lives. In a marriage, we all have our ups and downs, but as long as we keep Christ in the center of it all, he will always continue to guide us in love as we communicate with one another, in unity, and in obedience to the Lord. Our marriage is stronger than ever before, and we fervently work at it together and are victorious in our marriage. Through prayer and submission toward one another, we have defeated and overcome our enemy (1 Thessalonians 5:17 and Isaiah 54:17). Prayer has always been the key element to a successful marriage. It is the backbone of our faith, and we never leave home without it (2 Thessalonians 3:2-3). As Christians, we continuously remind the world and the devil that Christ is now the head of our lives, and he is our Lord. We like to remind Satan of his destiny and that the Lord Jesus is sending him right to hell (Revelation 20:10).

Our lives haven't been perfect, but the Lord sustains, strengthens, and protects us according to his promises, and has helped us through our struggles and afflictions. Marriage is a working progress that never ends, but Jesus is in the front seat stirring our lives and we have been cleansed by the blood of the Lamb (1 John 1:7).

Barbie and I still serve the Lord (Joshua 24:15). Praise the Lord!

A WORD OF ENCOURAGEMENT

I have been permanently disabled since 1999. I was first injured four months after I married Barbie while working in New Jersey. The date was February 1984, and we were having a blizzard storm. Due to this incident, I decided to return to school and refresh my skills and earned a certificate in secretarial skills. I had gone back to work after completing my course, and during the course of time, my physical ailment started acting up again, and on October 1997, I had surgery. At the time of surgery I was working for a state agency in New Jersey, and after three months, I returned to work. The problem continued to worsen, and finally my doctor decided I could no longer work in my condition. Next thing you know, I'm out of work permanently; I haven't worked a day since. A few years later I took two courses on biblical studies on the New Testament Survey at Somerset Christian College in New Jersey.

Why am I telling you this part of my life? Simple, I like you to know that even though I'm disabled, the Lord has made it cleared to me that life doesn't end just because of my severe condition. I have put all my trust in God, and Jesus has helped me overcome all my afflictions (Philippians 4:13). Satan tried to inflict me with depression, but with God's help, I have overcome the enemy and have become victorious in Christ the Lord. I still have physical pain, but I have God's love with me and his peace that sustains me. The Holy Spirit has strengthened me in a remarkable way through the reading of God's word. Had I not known the Lord, I would have been a big mess. I've had to do much praying and Bible reading in order to fight the spirit of depression and its demons. It's very easy to become depressed after having great health and then suddenly becoming disabled. But God is good and wonderful. I can honestly say to you that no matter what we go through, God is able, and we must trust him. He has filled me with his Spirit to the fullest and has enabled me to continued moving forward. For this reason, I praise God Ephesians 3:14–21).

Here's my point: Do not allow obstacles to get in the way of your dreams; fight back. If God is for us than who can be against us right? That's what the word of God teaches us (Romans 8:31). I pray that this inspires you to take charge of your life and say no to the devil. Stand firm in the faith and take the helmet of salvation, i.e., God's word according to Ephesians chapter six and apply it to your lives. God bless you!

I pray you can understand this and make the right decision for your life. Pickup your mat and walk in faith, and Jesus will always give you the victory. God bless you, thank you for reading my story, and may the Lord God bless you in His Son Jesus Christ, amen!

God in heaven had been watching it all from his heavenly throne. He knew Satan had the upper hand and even allowed the devil to take advantage of us, but in his mercy, he finally poured out his love towards our family. It took patience, prayers, fasting, pleadings and constant seeking his faithfulness, but he did it; he saved us. Maybe this is something hard for one to grasp, but God's love is infinite. He arrives in time and, at the end, always wins. Satan brought divisions among us and found loopholes to divide and destroy our family. But God had the final saying and a much bigger plan for us. No one saw it coming; not even

Satan. But God saved us all for his glory. Hallelujah, God is an awesome God.

I want to take this opportunity to first thank God, the Father of our Lord Jesus Christ for affording me the privilege of writing this book and this message. As an ambassador for Christ, I have brought you the good news of salvation. I could have not written this true story without the help of the Holy Spirit (Ephesians 2:10). Lord Jesus, please bless every soul that picks up this book to read it and afford them their salvations. Bless them Father, I asked you this in Jesus Christ name. Jesus is coming soon!

John writes in the New Testament, "We know also that the Son of God has come and has given us understanding, so that we may know him who is true. And we are in him who is true—even in his Son Jesus Christ. He is the true God and eternal life" (1 John 5:20, NIV).

The apostle John writes in the New Testament, "He who testifies to these things says, 'Yes, I am coming soon.'" Amen. Come, Lord Jesus. The grace of the Lord Jesus be with God's people. Amen" (Revelation 22:20–21, NIV).

Lord Jesus, I have conveyed your message…and this is your message.

> For God so loved the world that he gave his one and only Son, that whoever believes in him shall not perish but have eternal life. For God did not send his Son into the world to condemn the world, but to save the world through him. Whoever believes in him is not condemned, but whoever does not believe stands condemned already because he has not believed in the name of God's one and only Son.
>
> John 3:16–18 (NIV)

End of message!

Me and my siblings

My parents

My mother and my two oldest sisters

My father

My father

My mother

My sister Carmen

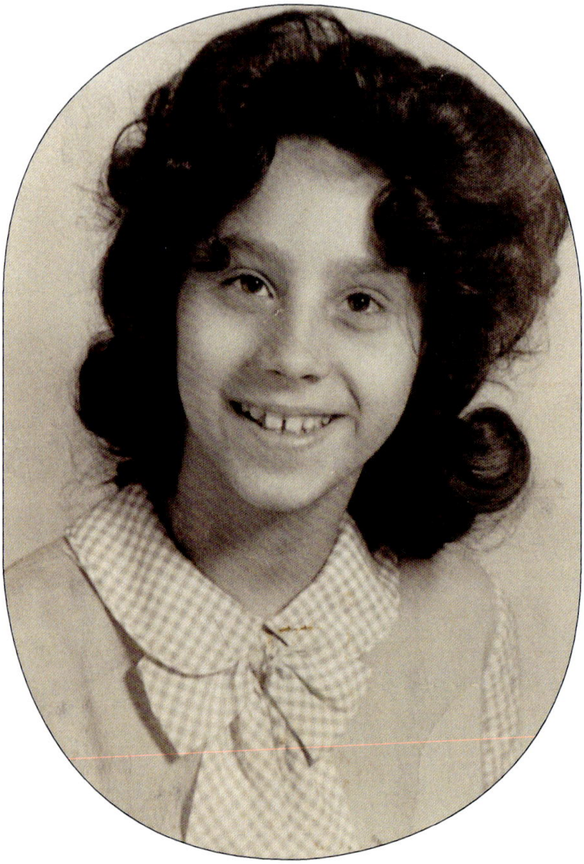

My sister Norma

My brother Jose

My sister Lourdes

My brother Carmelo

William

My sister Annette

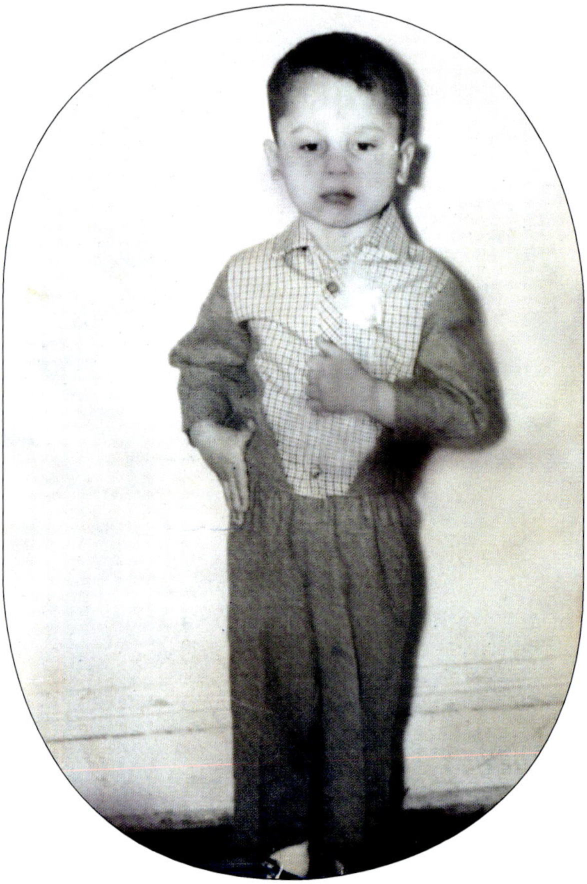

Me when I was three years of age

Me and my father Carmelo on my third birthday

Me and my mother Maria

Me, my mother Maria, and my sister Carmen

Me with my sisters Carmen and Annette with my mother Maria

Me with my brother Carmelo

My wife Barbara and me on our wedding day

My wife Barbara and me

Me and my wife Barbara

My parents with my brother Jose